Mirror
of our becoming

Praise for
Mirror of Our Becoming

"Ayres' poetic vision transforms ordinary perceptions into mystic beauty."
—Beatrice Bruteau, *The Grand Option* and *Radical Optimism*

"Lovely! Shows amazing breadth of thought!"
—Thomas Berry, *The Great Work* and *The Universe Story* (with Brian Swimme)

"The imagery is amazing. It took me back to my own childhood – I felt as if I were there, on the beach, laughing with friends and feeling the sea breeze. To actually feel this just from reading is quite the feat."
—MDDC Press Association

"This book has me remembering the rich pleasure of reading three essayists many years ago: Lewis Thomas, Loren Eisley, E.B. White."
—Rod Jellema, *Incarnality: The Collected Poems*

"One of the most poetic, beautiful love letters to the Chesapeake I have ever read."
—Ada Strausburg, the *Potomac Review*

"Most everybody in Chesapeake Country hears the poetry of wind and water, and many aspire to translate it into human language. Elizabeth Ayres succeeds. She startles us out of convention to think in new patterns."
—Sandra Olivetti Martin, *Bay Weekly* publisher and editor

Also by Elizabeth Ayres

Home After Exile:
A Spiritual Odyssey

Writing the Wave:
Inspired Rides for Aspiring Writers

Swimming the River of Stone:
Collected Poems

Creative Writing from A to Z
(audio book series)

Invitation to Wonder 'Journey' Series
(audio books)

For information on these titles please visit

www.CreativeWritingCenter.com

MIRROR
OF OUR BECOMING

MEDITATIONS ON NATURE'S BEAUTY, WISDOM AND MYSTERY

ELIZABETH AYRES

Veriditas Books

Copyright © 2014 by Elizabeth Ayres

Published by Veriditas Books
P. O. Box 968 • California, MD 20619
1-800-510-1049
VeriditasBooks.com • info@veriditasbooks.com

All rights reserved. No part of this book may be reproduced, stored in a retrieval system, or transmitted by any means, electronic, mechanical, photocopying, recording, or otherwise, without written permission from the author.

ISBN 13: 978-0-9845178-7-9
ISBN 10: 0-9845178-7-1
Library of Congress Control Number: 2014907128

Cover Design by Karen Phillips (www.phillipscovers.com)

Excepting "Fossils," "The Bridge," "The Comfort of Green," "Raindrops in the River" and "Still Night, Twin Moons" and excepting the essays noted below, the work appearing herein was first published in *The Enterprise* newspaper as a monthly column entitled "Soundings."

The following first appeared in *Bay Weekly*, the independent paper of Maryland's Annapolis capital region, in print and online (www.bayweekly.com). That publication's titles, when different from the author's, are indicated in parenthesis: "Bay Betrothal" ("The Pleasures of Summer"); "Passing By" ("The Passing of Maryland's Tobacco Calendar"); "Catching the Light;" "The Zone" ("The Swash Zone");" "The Work We Do" ("The Work We Do Is Ground Away"); "Thanksgiving Hallelujah" ("Preparing for Thanksgiving"); "The Journey" ("In One Sun's Setting Another Rises"); "Equinox" (Gallivanting on a Good Friday Full Moon"); "Blue Crab Etude;" "Remembering the Future" ("On Memorial Day"); "Sea Nettles;" "Berries, Blossoms, Bunting" ("Declarations of Independence"); "Vigil"("Celestial Navigation"); "Notes of a Native Daughter" ("Filling the Crater in Our Hearts").

to
my Chesapeake Bay homeland

"You called to me;
you shattered my deafness;
you put my blindness to flight."

– Augustine of Hippo, *Confessions*

Contents

Introduction 1

Spring

Prequel to 'Spring' 11
Song Flows Forth 13
Passing By 15
Equinox 17
Ghost Ship 19
Point of Intersection 21
Praising Green 23
Reconciling with April 25
What the Light Calls Forth 27
Maytime Musings 29
The Bridge 31
Remembering the Future 33
Seedsong: An Elegy 35

Summer

Prequel to 'Summer' 39
Bay Betrothal 41
The Comfort of Green 43
Barnacles and Tides 45

The Gift 47
The Pier 49
The Zone 51
Sea Nettles 53
Woodswalk 55
Blue Crab Etude 57
Butterfly Q & A 59
Berries, Blossoms, Bunting 61
The Gathering 63
Mimosa Moment 65
Secrets of Loveliness 67
Surrender to Solitude 69

Autumn

Prequel to 'Autumn' 75
The Work We Do 77
Knowing the Way by Water 79
Bones 81
A Slow and Gentle Easing 83
Raindrops in the River 85
Fossils 87
Vigil 91
Baking for the Holidays 93
Joe's Garden 95
Snow Geese and Other Considerations 97
Thanksgiving Reverie 99
Thanksgiving Hallelujah 101
The Moon of My Belonging 103
The Barn 105
In Praise of Surf 107

Winter

Prequel to 'Winter' 111
The Field 113
Catching the Light 115
The Fulcrum 117
Blue Moon 119
The Journey 121
Notes of a Native Daughter 123
Shadows 125
Everything Curves 127
Clouds 129
Cardinals 131
We Shall Be Changed 133
Keeper of the Light 135
A Different Kind of Wonderful 137
Rock Chorus 139
Still Night, Twin Moons 141
Deciphering the Season 143

A Message from the Author 145
Also by Elizabeth Ayres 148-151
Acknowledgements 153
Reader Discussion Guide 155
Study Guide for Writers 189
About the Author 203

INTRODUCTION

It used to be, I'd consult my mirror several times a day. Is my lipstick smudged? Is there spinach on my front tooth? Any new wrinkles or gray hairs? Sometimes I felt like Snow White's stepmother: "Mirror, mirror, on the wall, who's the fairest of them all?" I wanted my looking glass to tell me something terrific, something that would make me feel fabulous, and sometimes, in just the right mood, it might. Most of the time, though, I ended up with the same response that so enraged an evil queen. Until I traded up. Then, no matter how often I peered into its reflective surface, my mirror said, "You are beautiful. You are wise. You are loved."

I wrote this book to put my looking glass into your hands.

First, a little back story. I grew up in Chesapeake Bay country. Even before we lived there full time, our place on the water in Southern Maryland was our beach house. I loved it as a child, but as a teenager I hated it. It was so remote, and there were family tensions I needed to escape, so I left when I was 17 and rarely returned, even for brief visits. I lived most of my adult life in New York City, and then I lived in northern New Mexico. And all that time, I never really felt connected; I never really felt I had a home. I kept wandering around from place to place, lamenting my sad condition, my existential homelessness. I carried a deep sense of rootlessness and alienation which I suspect is rampant these days.

Finally, through a series of unexpected events, I ended up moving back to Southern Maryland. I wrote a monthly column for the local newspaper, focusing on the beauty, wisdom and mystery of the landscape, and the more I wrote, the more I realized that the place – especially the water – had been deeply imprinted on me during all those lost, rootless years. The connection to the place of my childworld just gushed forth onto the page every time I sat down to write, and the more I wrote, the less estranged I felt, until I came to realize, I do have a home after all. And because I have a home *here*, I have a home *everywhere*. It was a powerful experience of healing for me.

That's where the mirror comes in.

As I wrote the essays in this book, I began to experience myself in a new way. I carried my notebook around the seasons the way a landscape painter might lug an easel, and I came to understand on a visceral level that the life *around* me is the same as the life *within* me. I'm not separate from the whole. I'm part of it, I'm essential to it. Throughout history, humans have always found their deepest truth in Nature. But, with the rise of industry and technology, we have lost this simple truth, that the life *around* us is the same as the life *inside* us, because what surrounds most of us all day long? Staplers, paper clips, coffee machines, computers. They're inert; they can't tell us how to live, or why we should get up in the morning, or what it all means, if there's some purpose to our existence. Only the natural world, with its vibrant, vivifying energy, can show us who we really are, who we can become.

We Are Beautiful

When I was in college, our class read "Ode on a Grecian Urn" by John Keats. I clearly remember scoffing at those famous last two lines: "'Beauty is truth, truth beauty,' – that is all/Ye know on earth, and all ye need to know." How stupid, I thought. How can people say this guy's a great poet, when he's foisting nonsense off on us like something we can rely on?

I was young and angry. I wanted life to make sense – it didn't. I wanted certainty – none could be found. Keats' words disappointed me, epitomizing all the broken promises and frustrated hopes the world had so far proffered, so I marched off to find a more substantial truth.

Flash forward to now. I'm walking somewhere, and I'm startled by the vivid purple tips of a seed-blown thistle flower. Or maybe I'm driving, and the shape of a drifting cloud catches me off-guard. Or I'm sitting in my back yard, and some bird pipes up with a burst of song, and for one instant, I'm freed from my tiny self's illusory baggage of broken promises and frustrated hopes, catapulted to a place that's large and real and true. 'O, that's beautiful,' I think. And for that moment,

I know that the beauty in which I dwell is the truth that dwells within me. I have the courage to go on.

In the pages of this book, you will be mesmerized by a cardinal with its zing of red on a snow-clad branch. You'll be entranced by an old stump with its worn, pleated bark. You'll be intoxicated by a summer breeze, beguiled by April raindrops, spellbound by dawn, awed by sunset. You will know you are exactly that: mesmerizingly, entrancingly, beguilingly, intoxicatingly, spellbindingly, awesomely beautiful, and this knowledge will give you courage in times of trouble, profound satisfaction in times of joy.

We Are Wise

When I moved back to Southern Maryland, the place began talking to me. Every wave, every leaf, every bird, everything spoke to me, everything put words in my head. I called my monthly column "Soundings" – a nautical term for measuring the depth of water – because I wanted to get beyond some "tiptoe through the tulips" experience with the writing. I wanted to use my words to test the depth of my encounters with the natural world. I knew people would be reading the essays at a certain moment in time, so I used the existing structure of yearly holidays like warp threads on a loom. In the meditation called "Butterfly Q and A," for instance, I started out writing about honeysuckle. That was what was calling to me at the time, honeysuckle was in bloom, I was transfixed by the smell, but I also knew the column would appear in July, so I related it to Independence Day. Or in the reflection, "Vigil," I'd been wanting to write about the stars for a while. As Columbus Day approached I thought, 'Well, Columbus would have used the stars to navigate, so that's how I can link the two things together.' If the holidays were the warp threads, then the myriad reverberations with Nature became the weft, and gradually, over the course of four years, I realized I had somehow managed to weave myself securely into a strong, seamless fabric. I felt centered in a new and abiding way.

The dictionary says "wisdom" means "the exercise of sound judgment." But we can't judge anything rightly if we're disconnected from the whole, can we? In this book, you might find yourself in a skeletal wood, in winter. Amidst the serpentine twists and rope-like curves of bare tree limbs, you will learn that the fundamental architecture of any life is sound – despite, or even because of, its fits and starts, strides and missteps. That's wisdom, yes? That's something you can rely on when decisions must be made. Ambling along a beach in summer, in that dizzying zone where the tide's uprush and backwash meet, you might discover how your past desires and future needs are colliding. That's wisdom, yes? That's knowledge that can help you understand yourself and the people in your life, so you can act accordingly. Like any other mirror, Nature gives us critical information we might otherwise miss, and the reflections in this book can show you how to exercise your capacity for making decisions wisely, in harmony with that grand tapestry in which you are a single but essential thread.

We Are Loved

The psychologist Victor Frankl, a concentration camp survivor and author of *Man's Search for Meaning*, says that the people who survived the camps were those who had hope, who could tap into their connection to a loved one or to some larger purpose. Frankl said he survived because he could contemplate his beloved wife through all his trials.

My childhood was brutal, and I spent most of my life searching for love. Also for God, but scripture says, "God is love," so the two goals are really one and the same quest. I never felt loved, nor did I feel capable of offering love to anyone else – until I began writing about my Chesapeake Bay homeland. Then, with that notorious lover and Godseeker, St. Augustine of Hippo, I could finally say, "You called to me; you shattered my deafness; you put my blindness to flight." I've written about this experience extensively in *Home After Exile: A Spiritual Odyssey*, and won't try to summarize here. Just know that the reflections you're about to read were the hinges on a door that opened *in me* and *in front of me* at the same time.

A pivotal moment came while I worked on "In Praise of Surf." I was writing about waves, how they blur the boundary between in and out, then and now; how they are like two tines of a tuning fork, reverberating as one pure note. "Call it eternity, or infinity, or forever," I wrote. And then, without thinking, added, "Or call it love."

This shocked me. Waves on a beach? Love?

Another epiphany came as I worked on an essay about my friend's barn. I compared the red building to a heart, calling it "a tough, hard-working muscle." I said that when I'm inside her barn "the rafters of my own heart expand." And then added, "I shall set myself to the task of caring for this place of my belonging, this Earth, my only and every beloved."

This shocked me again. The Earth? My beloved?

Again and again, I found myself making these surprising connections between the natural world and what had, hitherto, been just an abstract idea for me. We say, "They knew each other in the biblical sense." We refer to sex as "carnal knowledge," because sex between two people who love each other integrates spirit and matter. It gives rise to an embodied knowing that goes beyond the abstract. Little by little, in my efforts to put into words my encounters with earth, sea and sky, I stumbled into a profoundly mysterious "carnal knowledge" wherein spirit and matter coalesced, opening me to give and receive love in my everyday relations with others.

The dictionary says love arises from recognition of attractive qualities or instincts of natural relationship. That it manifests as feelings of affection, attachment; as solicitude for the beloved's welfare, delight in the beloved's presence. You will experience a profound love for the world around you in the pages of this book. And as that mysterious door opens wider within and before you, you will learn that you and Love are just "two tines of a tuning fork, reverberating as one pure note." And if that's the case – if we're infinitely lovable, inexhaustibly loving, and inextricably entwined with Love's great purpose – how can we be anything but hopeful?

How to Use This Book

I've called these pieces "meditations," but they could just as easily be called "reflections" or "essays." They're very short – most are just 500 words – giving you a quick yet highly satisfying reading experience. My friend, Jane, says the book is like a box of chocolates. She says that as soon as she puts it down, she's looking forward to the next delicious morsel. So you could do as she does, just dive right in and start sampling.

Or give yourself a weekly vacation. The 59 reflections in the book are organized by season. If you were to read one each week, the book could happily carry you through an entire year, with a few treats left over for those times when you need an extra dose of inspiration.

I've also created a "Reader Discussion Guide." This is organized thematically, and every reflection in the book has at least three questions which will help you make the connection between my words and your own life experience. You'll even find suggestions for putting your encounters with Nature's beauty, wisdom and mystery into practice: individually, as a family, or as a member of any other life-enhancing group to which you belong.

Finally, I've included a special study guide derived from my online writing class, *The Writer's Eye: How to See with the Tip of Your Pen*. I've discovered, in the several years I've been leading the course, that literary skill – the creative manipulation of words to communicate thought and emotion – can be imparted almost by osmosis when aspiring writers pay close attention to how an accomplished artist achieves her effects. The questions in this section will reveal to the writer (or curious reader) the inner workings of the literary act, where, in the cauldron of the imagination, observation and insight meet.

In Conclusion

My friend, Kellie, gave me a butterfly garden for Christmas. Five caterpillars in a clear plastic cup. The tiny creatures exploded in size as they ate their way through the next week. Finally, one hung itself in a J-shape, upside down from the lid of the cup. Overnight, its skin hardened into a chrysalis, but the others couldn't make up their minds. They kept crawling around, up then down then up again, poking at the tough shell of their pioneering friend as if to say, "Me? That? You have *got* to be kidding!"

One by one, over the next few days, each caterpillar succumbed to the urge building up inside its own body: do this thing you've never done before; become something you can't even imagine. Even I, with my instruction book and my research, doubted that butterflies would emerge from those impenetrable black casings, but one morning, after I put the cup on a sunny window ledge, I saw one quiver. Six hours later, a Painted Lady butterfly was clinging to what had once been its own skin.

Its ruffled wings were orange, mottled with black, speckled with white dots. It had six fine, thin legs; two delicate antennae; one thread-like tongue it kept curling and uncurling, as if to test the use of this new body part. Indeed, while waiting for its wings to dry, the creature continually tried out all its new appendages. I could almost hear it thinking, "Me? This? You have *got* to be kidding!"

One by one, over the next few days, each of my butterflies discovered where instinct had taken it. And our instincts will take us to the same place, if we let them. We could do something we've never done before. Become something we can't even imagine. Because the beauty, wisdom and mystery in which we dwell is the truth that dwells within us. In whatever small way, I hope you'll discover your own truth in these pages.

SPRING

Prequel to 'Spring'

Yesterday. (You may start applauding now.) Yesterday, for the first time in some fifty years, I found a name for my first encounters with earth's fecund and seductive mysteries. I was three or four or five years old. Six or seven or eight, even, for this was a cyclic event, repeated every spring.

By late April, the exuberant yellow forsythia would have melted into green. ('For Cynthia,' my child-mind heard, envying that other little girl her bold and golden blossoms.) The pink and white bubbles of cherry, Bradford pear and dogwood would have burst, replaced by a thick, homogenous paste of green slathered onto every growing thing my myopic child-eyes could see. I loved to crawl into the dense sprawl of bushes behind our garage. On that little hill I would perch, lost in a derelict jungle, sheltered within a forgotten tangle of stems and branches and leaves that would sport luxuriant clumps of tiny white flowers which I loved to eat.

I can still taste them. I would place one morsel between my front teeth. Nibble. It was bitter, and crumbled unpleasantly on my tongue, yet I sampled another, then another, consuming who knows how many ounces or pounds of flowers in this, my first and holiest communion. We moved before I thought to seek a name for my efflorescent meal, but yesterday (Are you still clapping?), along the fence outside the public pool where I swim, ah, the tangled green sprawl of them, the profuse white bunches of them. "Do you know what those bushes are called," I asked the manager, and when she said, "No," I marched right out the door, snapped off a large branch, tossed it in my car and drove to the nearest nursery, whereupon fifty years of unknowing melted with George's confident proclamation.

"*Rosea banksia*," he declared, "Bank's rose." Then he grabbed a magnifying glass so I could see for myself. Yes, each tiny blossom resembled a miniature rose, a whorl of white petals, and beneath, a swirl of green sepals. "See," George said, handing the branch back to me, "It even has thorns."

We get a big charge out of naming things. What about Adam and Eve in the Garden of Eden? What about expectant parents? Last week, I went birding with a *bona fide* Audubon Society guide. My forest was filled with mysterious warbles, tweets and chirps. His forest was filled with birds, the names of which he rattled off while imitating their flight patterns with his hands. I was impressed, but not at all sure I wanted to trade my experience for his, because once you name a thing, once you fix it, pin it down, it becomes easy to substitute the word for the reality. When knowing crowds out unknowing, there's little space for wonder and delight.

Shall we, then, put aside this season's standard designation to walk through its days nibbling every derelict moment?

Song Flows Forth

No alarm needed to wake up these days, no sir, not with what those birds are doing outside my window every morning now. I'm not complaining, mind, I'm just saying: one day, silence, the next, wowie-zowie, spring is here, ushered in by a cacophony, a commotion, an uproar, ruckus, riot of singing. Of warbles, pipes, whistles, trills, twitters, tweets, chitters, chirps, cheeps, peeps and that's just my house, goodness knows what they're up to at yours.

I got curious. All that hubbub seemed so purposeful. I did a little fact finding and now I know some things I didn't know before. All year, male and female birds make calls. These are short, simple sounds used for short, simple reasons: warning, flight, distress. A song is different. It's a complex, melodious vocalization with repeated sections. Males sing, and only in spring, because the notes they're piping forth are meant for one purpose only: to claim a breeding area as their own and attract females to it. "Here I am," that's what they're saying. "Above all others, it's matchless me you want."

The songs of different species vary greatly in complexity and number. The humble Brown Thrasher has a repertoire of 2,000 distinct tunes, while the more spectacular American Goldfinch has just the one. Individuals within the same species differ as well. Starlings and mockingbirds create unique melodies for themselves by plucking bits and pieces from other birds' songs to weave into their own. They'll also borrow sound bytes from cows, cars, helicopters and chainsaws. Because young birds learn songs from their fathers, certain variations build up over generations, creating a distinct regional dialect. If you've been supposing that bird songs are shaped purely by instinct, suppose again, because the aria wafting its way to you right now is probably more individual artistic creation than species-specific program. Experiments with zebra finches prove that birds actually rehearse their songs in sleep, using their dream time to hone a whole range of improvisations they'll implement come dawn.

Spring is a lot like dawn, don't you think? In winter, the earth slips into a collective sleep. Identity is lost to sameness: bare branches, barren stalks, short syllables communicating common messages. Come the vernal equinox, everything bursts forth into its own special glory: cherry tree, forsythia, daffodil, all are warbling a singular song that says, "Here I am, matchless me, unique, distinctive, one-of-a-kind me."

And every dawn is another spring, don't you think? At night we abandon the hard shells of our separate identities to sink into the fertile alembic of the unconscious. There we pluck bits and pieces from a day, from a lifetime, from the whole broad range of human history. Come the morrow, we improvise. Not for us the ego's generic, utilitarian call of fight or flight, no, for each of us only the true song will do. Unique, distinctive, one-of-a-kind me flowing forth into that cacophony, that commotion, that riotous uproar called life or living, or is it just called singing after all?

Passing By

No shelter here. No defense against the wind that soughs across the weed-wracked field to do time's evil work: pry the rotting boards off. Peel the rusted tin away. Strip the flesh from this old tobacco barn, pick it clean to the bone.

Like a come-hither finger, it beckoned. Parking my car by the side of the road, I obeyed the summons. Now I stand, shivering, as slatted sunlight casts shadows to replace once-solid planks, and derelict hinges dream of swinging doors, and a medley of criss-crossed beams yearn to bear the fecund weight of tobacco leaves curing in the dark, rich air. Except now the brambles creep in, and the moss, and whatever wild and profuse promptings cultivation holds at bay.

I remember how they were when I was a child, these early springtime fields. The white cloth spread like giant wings to protect the fragile seedlings huddled underneath. The plowed and patient earth, her furrows flung out like arms waiting to embrace June's adolescent transplants.

We weren't farmers, but in those days, tobacco was the staple crop of Southern Maryland, and month by month the growing of it strung taut warp threads of recurring sights on a year's loom. Almost shoulder height by late summer. September's workers in the rows, cutting the stalks, spearing them onto stakes, carting the skewered harvest into the barns to be hung on tiered poles to dry. December's secrets I learned from kids who missed school to stand for long hours inside those mysterious, gambrel-roofed hives, where they stripped and bulked and barreled the brown stuff. Then the beat-up trucks and horse-drawn Amish carts headed for Hughesville and the auction house.

We weren't farmers, but our everyday shuttlings – to store, school, church, doctor's office – flashed like many-hued weft threads through a fabric larger than any mere comings or goings. Harvests and earth and weather. A pristine, primal tapestry to remind us we are all just seeds in our season.

I wasn't here for the 2001 Buyout, when the state offered tobacco growers money to switch to other crops. Now I'm back, and like everyone else I see the barns won't survive the transition. Inside, they're filled with heavy rafters crosshatching a maze of small compartments. All that can be stored there is the hanging brown weed they were built to hold. Who can afford to maintain buildings that no longer serve a purpose? They rot where they stand.

This day, rusted bolts pepper the ground. Twisted shags of tin tumble from a fraying roof. White bones of vapor trails litter a sapphire sky. Cars roar by where silence once reigned, and some kid hunkers down in the abandoned field. His remote-controlled model airplane buzzes round and round in a noisy, futile circle. Buzzes round and round, treading the same worn out path.

Soon, the great religious feasts of spring will be upon us. Passover. Blood on wooden doorposts, the houses empty, their occupants fled in terrified hope to seek a future they name the Promised Land. Easter. Blood on a wooden cross, the empty tomb, its occupant come forth to tell us: we are all seeds in our season. This day *is* the Promised Land.

Last night I dreamt I was hoeing tobacco. I could hear them laughing, the men who built this barn. Who pounded in the shiny nails and thought their shiny thoughts for a new harvest. The auction house is closed now, but that's no never-mind, spring is here again, her come-hither finger raised, and yes, it's sad those old buildings are crumbling, but this I know from religion and the season: it isn't loss that defines us. Death is a question mark, not an exclamation. And while I can't say what question you might hear it ask, "Who stands at this day's door, knocking?" is the invitation I'll hear whispered every time I'm passing by some old tobacco barn.

Equinox[*]

It meandered, the path. It snaked through a tangled skein of bare trees and I followed. Twisting where it twisted close to the river. Winding where it wound close by a field. It made me giddy, that trail. Made me leave behind plain old mundane hiking to gallivant, gad about, knock around. Lighthearted, I forgot what was: a dull, cold day in early March, and remembered to keep watch for what could be.

The old stump with its worn, pleated bark. What if I were to pluck it up and play it like an accordion? The velvet, chartreuse moss. What if I were to fling it around my shoulders like a cape? Maybe I'm not even walking forward, I thought, maybe I'm climbing upwards on a haphazard trellis of exposed roots. Or swimming. The rippled, wavy lines etched into the naked pith might be from some current or tide.

No surprise, when the downed dead tree spoke. With its ruffled frills of peeling bark stained green by lichen. With olive-striped butterfly wings of fungus fluttering along its length. The tree said, "Dying, I destroyed death, for see the life I've reinvented?"

Those words come back to me now, as I look to where the meandering path has brought us. Snaking through a tangled skein of days. Twisting. Winding. See? Already it is the vernal equinox, when light and dark are perfectly balanced. Tomorrow, the full moon, when waxing and waning briefly halt their ceaseless motion. Then Easter Sunday. Commemorating death's destruction and the reinvention of life.

It's making me downright giddy, this mighty confluence of forces, for see? It's leap year. Earth takes 365.25 days to go around the sun; so every four years we must disappear that stockpile of extra hours. February 29th is an anchor we cast out to stop calendar dates from

---

[*] Author's note. This was published on Thursday, March 20, 2008; hence, the very specific numerical calculations.

drifting through the seasons. And see? Easter is always the first Sunday after the first full moon after March 21st, which moon occurs tomorrow: Friday, March 21st. This date is usually the first day of spring unless it's had to leap with the year, back to March 20th, which happens to be the day I'm writing. Easter has fallen on March 22nd only four times since the Gregorian calendar was adopted in 1582. It won't occur on March 22nd until 2285. Easter has come on March 23rd just 6 times, and after this coming Sunday, it will be 2160 before these two meet again.

It's enough to make us abandon the mundane, don't you think? 2008 is special, a gallivantin', gad about, knock around kind of year. I say we leap beyond what is – that horrid war, for instance – and keep watch for what could be. As they will Saturday night, during the Easter Vigil, extinguishing all light then rekindling the new fire. As earth does every year, all outward growing extinguished, then all the green rekindled. What if all the killing stopped? Wouldn't that be our downed dead reinventing themselves as peace? Wouldn't that be like someone expiring because they've been nailed to a tree, then later saying, "Dying, I destroyed death, rising, I restored life."

All the moons have names, you know. Depending on the tradition you follow, you might call tomorrow Big Famine Moon, because game is scarce. Or Sap Moon, because the time for tapping maple trees is here. Or Crust Moon, because the snow thaws by day and freezes at night. Or Worm Moon, because earth worms are astir now, and robins.

Depending on your tradition, you might call tomorrow Good Friday. This, to my way of thinking, is a kind of anchor. An event cast out into the cosmos to stop our inexorable drift towards extinction. Whether you believe that or not, there is still cause for lighthearted rejoicing. See? The tundra swans are leaving for their Arctic breeding ground, and the osprey are returning. Winter and spring, dark and light, death and life – all these mighty forces balance out today. And tomorrow then tomorrow then tomorrow tip the scales.

Ghost Ship

Someone told me she'd been sunk at a nearby marina, and now she's mysteriously appeared in Mill Cove, her once white hull stained and splotched, her anchor line slack, dispirited. She looks to me like a work boat, like she spent her whole life in hard service to some waterman, who spent his whole life plowing the bay's bittersweet furrows for its harvest of crabs and oysters.

As I sit on a log half listening to the susurration of high tide slipping and sliding into the reedy stalks of marsh grass, the hard edge of what was softens, blurring into what might have been. I see her flaunting a jaunty, white-plumed wake, dashing out into the Atlantic then down to the Bahamas. Her captain and crew toss aside their work clothes to don swim trunks and scuba gear. They splash into warm, sapphire depths where multi-hued fish help them explore coral reefs and shipwrecks. At night, the boat smiles blissfully, moored among fat yachts and sleek sail boats, her men off somewhere, laughing, slugging back exotic rum drinks, singing calypso, dancing the limbo.

Sure, and don't you agree? There is some deep hunger at the heart of all matter to be more than, to break free of, whatever constraints its form currently imposes. When we had that big snowfall in February, I found an old tree trunk stranded on the beach, its long-dead roots encased in ice which had melted, re-frozen, melted again, until crystalline stalactites pierced the sand, growing the tree into a new and watery life it never could have imagined until I came along and saw its inarticulate yearning, its groping to become more than, to break free of the constraints death had imposed on it, just as I have imagined this ghost ship into a whole new existence, and I'm wondering if this might be the gift we humans are meant to bestow on the Earth, on each other. Call it Easter, or Passover. Call it Resurrection, or Exodus. Call it imagination or vision or intuition. Call it whatever you will, each of us can do it.

Suppose, for example, you could look at your ornery, obnoxious cousin or brother or boss or neighbor until those hard edges softened and you could glimpse a yearning to be kind or reasonable or generous. Wouldn't that momentarily free someone from slavery to greed or anger or whatever? Or suppose you could look at the Earth until the boundaries separating individual objects blurred and you could no longer even say, there's a pine tree, there's a river, there's a fish, no, because you see the deep hunger at the heart of all these things to be one living, thriving, pulsing, begetting being, and if you could do that, wouldn't the Earth then smile blissfully, having sailed us away from the ghostly existence we are trapped in to the new and fuller life she has always imagined for us? Wouldn't we all be laughing and singing and dancing then?

Point of Intersection

On any other day I could not do this: could not walk this beach past the tidal pool, its entrance a deep wide gash that obstructs the path of all but the most agile of jumpers or determined of waders. I am neither, especially when burdened with coat and boots, but today the wind-driven tide is so low it has stitched both sides of the watery wound together with sand, and I am free to continue on, carefully pressing my footprints – one, then another, then another – next to the tracks of a raccoon, until, alongside my unseen precursor, I arrive here, where I've never been, to sit on a log and savor this unaccustomed perspective on a familiar scene.

Other tracings on an otherwise unscathed shore. Scalloped ripples made by currents and waves. A herringbone pattern where wind and surf collided. A zigzag rivulet made by water trickling into Mill Creek around a mussel shell embedded in the sand. Everything seeks its proper route through life, and everything meets resistance. I trudged through deep snow to get to the beach today. Saw trees bent low and bushes flattened by a crystalline burden that shimmered, gem-like, in the sun. Heard wind churn through shuddering pines. So many, my own burdens, so frequent, the bitter gusts. Yet, the rainbow sparkle. Yet, the ineffable song.

Twice each year there comes a moment of pure and unutterable balance. The equinox. When Earth's axis tilts neither from nor towards the Sun, which is passing directly over the Equator. If, suspending their quarrel, day and night can equal each other in length, then perhaps there's hope for other forces of opposition. I affirm this daily, whenever I pause at the intersection on Route 235. A right, and Shady Mile Lane will take me back to the house where I grew up. A left, and Old Rolling Road will take me to the house I live in now. It's the same stretch of pavement, though. An asphalt, seesaw reminder that there can be equilibrium between present and past.

Now we have this seasonal pause at the intersection of the year. Light and dark: different names for time's one road. What if, just briefly, we could call it neither gift nor curse, could shrink not from nor stretch out towards the event, the situation, the circumstance. What if, briefly, we could suspend ourselves above all judgment and allow the deeper truth to reveal itself in each moment of our life? Like those first astronauts who, hurtling beyond the familiar constraints of gravity and atmosphere, arrived someplace they had never been before. Paused. Looked back to Earth. Saw that the separations we believe exist vanish when viewed from a distance. Sitting here on this beach, I believe it must be possible. For me, for you, for all of us, with our quarrels, our many names for the one road. All forces of opposition can find a balance. The equinox tells us so.

PRAISING GREEN

Like a kid kept after school to repeat her lessons (I must not talk in class, I must not talk in class), spring's return has me filling in the blank lines of every day's page with endless variations on one simple theme: green, green, green, green, green, green, green. Everywhere I go, everywhere I look: green, green, green, green, green, green, green.

Green grass. Green trees. Green bushes. Green in long thin skewers, fat round dollops. Green edges serrated, green edges smooth, spiked green needles with no edges at all. Close up, green can prickle or feel soft to the touch. From a distance, green is an immensity in which I lose myself. An infusion in which I can steep. A silence into which I am gathered.

Green is strong and stalwart, reliable, but green keeps secrets, don't you think? There's some espionage going on between green and the season. To discover what it is, I turn to the book spring provides. Green. Chapter One. Chlorophyll needs every color in the spectrum except green, which it generously bequeaths to our human eyes. Chapter Two. Chlorophyll 'b' absorbs more red than chlorophyll 'a,' which makes it go ga-ga. Chapter Three. Concerned that chlorophyll 'a' might feel cheated, chlorophyll 'b' shares its energy. Chapter Four. Chlorophyll 'a' is happy and grateful. To show its appreciation, it gets to work making something chlorophyll 'b' can't make: sugar. Something we humans can't make, either: oxygen. Chapter Five. The chemical compound that stores sugar and releases oxygen in plants is similar to the chemical that forms DNA in people, who exhale the carbon dioxide plants inhale to keep making the sugar we eat and the oxygen we inhale.

Ah, I understand now, yes, that explains it. Why I want to call green my home. Why I want to fall into green as if into a dear friend's arms. Why I want to croon green jazz all night long, until morning comes and I can see my sweet and precious green once more. We are soul mates, lovers, life partners.

Green inspires me, completes me, challenges me to be my best. Is there someone who doesn't have something I have a lot of? I'll share, like chlorophyll 'b.' Do I have some special gift? I'll use it to make the world a better place, like chlorophyll 'a.' I'll be everything my beloved green calls me to be: a perfection of give and take, an apotheosis of cooperation, and while I'm at it, I'll see what I can do about those fossil fuel emissions. People are putting out more carbon dioxide than green can take in, and we don't want to become the parasite in this wonderful symbiosis, do we? Because that would sort of be like two-timing a soul mate, not to mention giving the book a very sad end.

So I think I'll stay right here, praising green, green, green, green, green, green, green, until I'm blue in the face.

Reconciling with April

I asked April, "What do you think about yesterday's front page news?" She said, "Yes!" Then I queried, "When will the current war be over?" She replied, "Yes!" I pressed again. "What's going on with the economy?" She answered, bright and cheery, "Yes!"

April obviously has a one-track mind when it comes to the sociopolitical scene, so I got personal, raising an issue she couldn't possibly sidestep. "What about that?" I screamed, naming my deepest hurt, but she just smiled. "Yes!" So I called forth my second deepest hurt, then the next, then the next, a litany, an armada of wounds. I named all mine then started in on yours: abandonment, betrayal, sickness, addiction, I even made up some troubles no one's ever heard of before, but she just kept grinning, "Yes! Yes! Yes!" that's all she would say.

Exasperated, I turned my back on the month of April and went outside, slamming the door behind me so she would get the message. She'd be sorry. She'd feel guilty. And I'll never apologize first, I said to myself, hopping in my car, turning on the ignition, she'll have to beg and plead. I backed up, narrowly missing three foolish children playing hopscotch – hopscotch! – in the parking lot. They'd marked up the nice neat blacktop with a lot of bright, cheerful colors. That'll show them, I thought, driving over their board, although as I sped off I checked in the rear view mirror and sure enough, they'd defiantly regrouped to resume their silly game, as if what I'd done didn't matter. Plucky brats, resilient, just as irritating as April, I'll show them all.

I drove around, determined to remember all my grievances for when I got back to the house to have it out with April, but then I made a mistake: I rolled down my window. I heard the peepers, Earth herself crooning to comfort a fretful babe. I smelled spring onions, a warm, scented oil rubbed into dry, cracked skin. I noticed how the green was spreading like a thick, healing salve. How forsythia, daffodil, phlox, cherry, all had defiantly returned to play hopscotch – hopscotch! – on the forsaken land. Plucky. Resilient. As if what winter had done didn't really matter.

"Yes," I muttered, grudgingly, as I passed a garden spangled with pansies. "Yes," I whispered, hesitantly, as I admired the lime-green fountain of a nearby willow. "Yes!" I exclaimed, downright exuberantly, when a shy dogwood peeped out from behind a sheltering pine. That's when I finally heard her. April. Begging me to pay attention, pleading with me to practice with her the one word that can make the difference between winter and spring, between grievance and possibility, between politics-as-usual and genuinely responsible leadership.

But don't take my word for it, test it out right now. Try "Yes!" like chalk on the blacktop of your despairing heart. Keep practicing until I come back, I have to run now, I have to find April and apologize.

What the Light Calls Forth

The year is waxing, like the moon. From the dark and secret jug of night, the pointillist song of frogs spills forth. Urgent. Insistent. Pressing on the shell of darkness as if to crack it open, and every vernal pool and ditch now swells with the get of frogs: luminescent, gelatinous orbs a-quiver with new life.

The Welsh have a phrase, *pwdre ser*, 'rot of the stars.' Makers of legend and poetry claim that shooting stars leave behind a fetid, shining jelly whenever they strike the ground. The English call it 'star slough,' the French, *crachat de la lune*, or 'spit of the moon.' Scientists say it could be any number of minute organisms: slime molds, fungus, bacteria, all of which can produce shimmering, viscous clumps of color which excitable folk might stumble upon in pastures or forests where meteorites reportedly have crashed.

Scientists also say matter is slow-moving light. That is, matter sometimes acts like particles, existing at particular points in space, but sometimes acts like waves, cohering as vibrational patterns. My head can't wrap itself around these facts, but my heart whispers, "I knew it all along." We are all little moons, waxing and waning in response to the sun, which is present in every photon-bearing atom on the planet. Come tomorrow's Maytime dawn, the splash of birdsong will fill morning's bucket, the willow will pour greenly to earth, and every yellow or red or purple flower will spurt from its small green cup.

Come tomorrow, the light will unstopper night's dark and secret jug, releasing me from encumbering failures and torturous guilt, spilling me forth into the day along with birds and trees and flowers. The light will whisper, "It is I, it is I, it is I," and my heart will answer, "I knew it all along," for such is the destiny of all creation, to be one in the light.

I hear people talk about their vocation as if it were nothing more than their occupation, what they do to make a living. That's way far down the list of definitions, if you look the word up in the *Oxford English Dictionary*. There you'll see that the Latin *vocare* means to call or summon, and for generations people have understood a vocation to be a divine beckoning. Maybe this is why poets and mythmakers have been so eager to find evidence of extraterrestrial life in the shining jellies found in field or forest where some shooting star might have lain. We ourselves are star slough, spit of the moon. Carbon, nitrogen, oxygen, fashioned in the sun's explosive, gaseous womb, then released to press on the shell of darkness as if to crack it open. Every pool and ditch, every mountain and valley, every animal, mineral, vegetable swelling with the get of stars: carbon, nitrogen, oxygen in myriad arrangements of vibrating photons, a wholeness that the light calls forth, that beauty and truth proclaim, that omniscience asks us to know and omnipotence summons us to create.

Maytime Musings

A knot is what it is, my heart, and when it needs untying, I walk in the woods, or ramble along the shore, or stride through some meadow under an open sky, it doesn't matter where, any door takes me to the place I need to be.

Home. Where someone will shower my bruised soul with soft whispers and sweet kisses: the sound of small wild things scraping in the underbrush, or the touch of a gentle breeze on my face, or the tender, glassine caress of waves on sand.

My mother. Who knows me better than I know myself, and speaks my true name when everyone else has forgotten, and answers life's triune interrogatories: who are you, what do you want, where are you going?

Who am I? I am this immensity, this tangled profusion of living, breathing, growing, changing. My name is sycamore, sassafras, sweet-gum. If you call out to the wind-borne gull or hawk, I will answer.

What do I want? To be free. To dwell beyond the reach of mechanism and artifice, task and successful execution thereof, because beyond all formulation of petty desires there is the great, round wheel: spring, summer, autumn, winter, spring, summer, round and round, an ancient purpose, my only necessary commitment.

Where am I going? I do not know, and I do not want to know, but for this adventure I will need courage that rises like sap. And the exuberant, spontaneous wisdom possessed only by things that arrive at beauty through routes wild, uncultivated, unplanned.

A knot is what it is, my heart, and when it needs untying I go home to Mother. Who tells me what I need to hear: I can never be satisfied or content except with something greater than myself. When I feel worn and tossed about, like some little scrap of cloth, Mother's truth is a sharp needle, it flashes in and out, it stitches me back into the fabric of earth and sea and sky. When I'm frightened, Mother assures me all shall be well, and all manner of thing shall be well. For Mother's consoling presence I am thankful. Nor can my gratitude be measured by any instrument known in space or time. It is infinite. Like her. Through whom we all came to be.

Hallmark makes no cards for this, but Mother herself provides us with the perfect celebration: the month of May. Think of all those flocks, herds, hosts, packs, droves, drifts, swarms, covies. Skulks of foxes, clowders of cats, gams of whales, skeins of geese, charms of finches. All that progeny, issue, offspring, that hatching, spawning, whelping, those broods, gets, litters, clutches, farrows, sons, daughters.

Somewhere in all of that, you and I. Who are we? This immensity. What do we want? Alignment with this great purpose. Where are we going? We don't know, but for such an adventure, let's all ask Mother for courage. And the wisdom to journey by her preferred routes – those that are wild and unplanned.

THE BRIDGE

Long and thin and white, it curves across the lower Patuxent like a gull's wing. At its midpoint, it is 20 feet higher than the river is deep. At its midpoint, I am launched forth above broad waters into an open sky, free as flight itself. At its midpoint, travelers are suspended between two Maryland counties, and anyone who wants can listen to the bridge speak. *That which was divided is now made whole*, it says, in its native tongue of spinning wheels and axles, passengers and freight.

When I was growing up – on Mill Creek in St. Mary's County – Solomon's Island, in Calvert County, was a 10 minute jaunt by boat, or a 90 minute trek by land. Now I can make the drive in five minutes. Every trip across the 1.4 mile strip of concrete gives me the thrill of doing something that wasn't possible before, and I love to hop in my car and toodle on over to the Solomon's Island boardwalk. The bridge dominates the view from here. Busy and industrious, people hurtle northbound on Route 2/4, zoom southbound with efficiency, purpose. Doing what wasn't possible before. Easy access to the Navy base for Calvert County residents. Easy access to the Baltimore-Washington corridor for folks in St. Mary's County. Jobs. Tourism. Commerce. The bridge makes the Patuxent River the spine of a butterfly. Hitherto separate entities on either side of her shores can now rise up, flap their wings together, fly forth as one into a prosperous future.

But progress has its downside. The sound of rubber wheels slapping on asphalt intrudes on my boardwalk reverie, so I retreat back across the bridge to a favorite riverside park. Here, I can sit on a spit of sand, back nestled against the cliffside, embraced by gnarled roots, serenaded by insects and birds. Incoming waves break gently on logs slick with seaweed, peppered with barnacles. Sunbeams glance off the water's surface like Morse code. Those dots and dashes of light signal nothing to no one, or everything to anyone willing to decipher the message. If I were to wade in and stay there, my skin would wrinkle up like the rippled sand of the shallow breakwater, where tide and current conspire to leave a track of their wanderings.

Industry, yes. Beetles scuttle every which-way across the sand, purposeful in their chaotic scrambling. An osprey swoops down, glides away with a fish in its talons, and for just an instant, the curve of its one wing in the foreground merges perfectly with the arc of the bridge in the background. The crabbers are out, their work boats lined up like horses at the starting gate, the floats on their trot lines bobbing up and down like little ducks.

Last week, driving home from here, I rescued a turtle as it tried to cross the road. When I pulled over to get out of my car, the bridge in the distance seemed to give me a conspiratorial wink. It was just an ordinary eastern box turtle, helmet-shaped, splotched brown and yellow. I picked him up, he disappeared into his shell, but as I neared the grassy roadside, his head and legs poked out and he began a furious mid-air crawl. His eyes were fiercely intent on escape, and my heart melted with pity for the creature, so determined to fix his own destiny, so utterly helpless in my hands.

The Governor Thomas Johnson Bridge is white, like oyster shells bleaching in the sun. White, like periwinkles glistening on broad green blades of sea grass. It trumpets itself across the Patuxent River, majestic tribute to possibility, change, progress. Laudable purposes all, but not the real reason the bridge was built. No, this graceful sweep of steel and concrete exists so that, if ever there should be an accident at the Calvert Cliffs Nuclear Power Plant, people living below it in the southern tip of Calvert County will be able to escape southbound across this extension of Route 2/4, into St. Mary's County, hence to points north. Like that determined, helpless turtle?

Remembering the Future

Like a bayonet brandished against the tide, the long, thin peninsula that is St. Mary's County, Maryland tapers to a sharp tip at Point Lookout, where the Potomac River meets the Chesapeake Bay. When I visited in early March, the day itself was at arms. A tearing wind that flattened beach grasses and twisted tree branches. Clouds heaped in the sky like heavy, gray boulders. An angry white surf clawing at the sand. Small wonder that the elements assail each other there, given the history of the place.

During the American Revolution, it was a lookout whence spies reported on the British fleet. Next there came the lighthouse. Next there came the resort, with a hotel, wharf and cottages. Pleasure seekers vanished when the Civil War erupted, so next there came the hospital, built to treat Union soldiers then expanded to incarcerate ever-increasing numbers of Confederates. Next there came the prisoner of war camp, but the prisoners needed guarding, so three forts were built, and in the midst of it all, a contraband camp evolved, refuge for African Americans escaping from southern captivity to northern liberty.

Such bald, bare facts. But what about the lives torn, flattened, twisted? Some 5,000 men, women and children died at Point Lookout. In Hammond Hospital, with its 16 spoke-like wings, its 1,400 beds a revolving wheel of pain for those laid low by bullets, bombs, shrapnel, disease. In Camp Hoffman, where, over the course of two short years, 52,000 Confederate soldiers were walled up, living in tents, with scant rations, in every extreme of weather, suffering from malaria, dysentery, smallpox. In the Contraband Camp, where hungry, frightened folk burrowed into dens in the damp earth "like beasts of the field," one appalled nurse reported.

And in the forts? That day in March, I roamed through the reconstructed barracks of Fort Lincoln. Thin plank walls kept the wind out, but not the cold. In summer, it would have been an oven. I imagine I am a soldier of the 5th Regiment, stationed here as guard. I peer through the window, out over the earthen ramparts, to the Potomac flowing freely under an open sky. Home is somewhere out there, my wife, my children, my ease. Duty has brought me to this place of constant worry. Is that the wind roaring or cannon fire? Waves on sand or the enemy's boots? It's gall I eat with my daily bread, this perpetual fear of attack.

In 1867, Nella Sweet published a hymn, "Kneel Where Our Loves are Sleeping," dedicated "To the Ladies of the South who are Decorating the Graves of the Confederate Dead." This grassroots ritual morphed into Decoration Day, when flowers were placed on the graves of Union and Confederate soldiers, then morphed again into Memorial Day, which honors Americans who have died fighting in any war. Perhaps we'll call it something else in the future, if we ever wake up long enough to realize: all our loves lie sleeping somewhere, this whole planet should be festooned with flowers.

That blustery afternoon in late winter, I met Bob, a member of the group that's been restoring Point Lookout's historical sites. Two of Bob's ancestors were imprisoned in Camp Hoffman, and he served in Vietnam. We spoke of war, and duty, and I wandered off, down to the beach, where I found a clutch of feathers, the tattered remains of some unlucky bird's free flight. I thought, On my mother's side, my Georgia forbearers could be buried here; on my father's side, my German Jewish kin could be buried at Dachau; if I had had children, they might have died in Iraq. That's when it came to me, we are all prisoners of war, and according to the Geneva Convention, it's our duty to escape.

Now, Memorial Day. Would it not honor those who have died in our wars, to spend one moment contemplating peace? Peer through the window, over the ramparts? It's somewhere out there, and the taste of bread without the gall, if only we could fly free of this place where, just now, we all seem to be stationed.

Seedsong: An Elegy
for Thomas Berry, 1914-2009

The day we said goodbye to you, a loon sang on a blue lake as clouds separated into white islands dotting a blue lake of sky. Shovels bristled in the mound of black earth heaped beside your open grave, and mountains leaned into each other like sorrowing friends. In the garden, seedlings bristled in their own black earth. Then a long line of friends filed past a fragrant stand of balsam pines into the meadow. Then it was done, and we all went home.

It takes time to hear the voice of a place. I think you might have said that, although they could be my words, or this woodsy fringe of the Chesapeake Bay swelling into thought – sometimes the connections blur the distinctions, and I can't tell the difference. This place speaks in the creaking wings of an unseen gull, its gray body blending into the gray mist as a dream blends into sleep. As Earth's dream winged its way into your sleep and, waking, you woke us all. There are no words on the boulder that is your headstone, but it's been calling to you since you were a child, that meadow, in its mother tongue of lilies and crickets, its alphabet of white clouds dotting a blue sky.

White mushrooms dot the wet green grass here. I stand on a sodden carpet of pine needles. A network of exposed roots meanders, like the ropey veins on an old man's hands. That one time I met you, we read to each other. From your work, from my work, from the work of a host of friends, all those words, thoughts, visions, dreams, all falling

---

* Author's note. Thomas Berry was a priest, scholar, cultural historian, author and (a word he coined to combine geology with theology) geologian. His books include *The Dream of the Earth* and *The Universe Story* (with Brian Swimme). Berry taught us to see the universe as "a communion of subjects, not a collection of objects." His vision was deeply informed by a childhood experience in a meadow, described in another of his seminal books, *The Great Work*.

like droplets of rain, mingling, overflowing, seeping into the ground, absorbed, transformed, and look, Thomas, look! How the pine trees have flung their seed-laden cones with such reckless generosity.

Look, Thomas. In the sweet salt wind, storm clouds roil and boil, seethe and churn. White as lilies, black as crickets, every shade of gray in between. The bright light and the dim light, the shine and the shade, borne in each other's arms, waltzing across the sky. I do not know what happens after we die, but I do know there is some mysterious exchange between creation and annihilation, between possibility and the extinction thereof. I know this mystery is choreographed into the structure of galaxies and grains of wheat, and that we are all partners in the dance, and that the single yellow dandelion blooming near my foot will soon become a gossamer white globe. Then the gust of wind, and a thousand seeds flying on a thousand gossamer wings.

It takes time to hear the voice of a place. From north and south and east and west, a thousand gossamer stories, borne on the wind like seeds. Sun and moon, mountains and meadows, lilies and crickets and stars – you taught us to listen, Thomas, and to speak the truth of our own story in the vocabulary of our mother tongue. A language with no word for 'goodbye.'

SUMMER

Prequel to 'Summer'

Where the Atlantic Ocean thrusts her salty fist into North America's eastern seaboard (Maryland, Virginia, Delaware, we call them) – that's the Chesapeake Bay. Where the Bay, in turn, wriggles two long salty fingers into Maryland – that's the Potomac and Patuxent Rivers. And where the Patuxent River tickles St. Mary's County with a salty pinkie – that's Mill Creek, where I grew up.

I learned to swim before I could walk, so it's no surprise that summer and water are inextricably linked for me. I remember my parents, standing chest high in the sun-sparkled creek while I dogpaddled back and forth between them. I remember my father diving down, my arms wrapped around his neck, then he would surface, laughing. "Wasn't that wonderful?" he would shout, and I would giggle my agreement. I remember mermaid tea parties underwater, and playing with the barnacles that encrusted our pier pilings, and the long, lonely half-hour wait after every meal, before I could get back to the element that felt so natural and welcoming.

The first time I saw the ocean, I plunged right in. I saw the other kids body-surfing – that seemed easy enough – but a slight miscalculation put me under, not on top of, a breaking wave. It dragged me under, churned me around, wouldn't let go until it flung me high up on the beach, gasping for breath, with scraped knees and a bathing suit filled with sand. The sea, I had learned, could be an alien, unfriendly realm.

There was a frog living in our swimming pool. The pool was old and crumbling – too expensive to fix. Clotted with dead leaves and stagnant rainwater, it became home to a rather stentorious and long-lived creature about which the neighbors teased my father. "That old bullfrog of yours, keeps me up half the night," they would mock-complain. But they didn't understand, and how could I explain, that every night he sang me down into his amphibian world, where water is our natural element and dreams a welcome form of awareness. Perhaps in this next set of reflections, you and I and that old bullfrog will sing ourselves into summer's magical realm.

Bay Betrothal

Ocean waves are horses with foaming mouths, ridden by witches wielding reins of seaweed. So say the Mapuche people of Chile, and who should know better? On a map, their land looks like a long thin blade of seagrass flung shoreward by the vast Pacific. Waves could be an angry Na-maka-o-kaha'i, Hawaiian goddess of the sea. Or a capricious Neptune, prodding at the surface with his trident to make a spot of trouble for some sailors.

Such stories came to me yesterday as I paced a shell-strewn beach, plucking at words, trying to describe to myself the look of sunlight on the Chesapeake Bay's wind-ruffled water. Gleam, glitter, sparkle? No, jewels are too inert. Dance, laugh, play? That's better, more alive, but what about awe and reverence for something totally beyond, utterly other? Something I can never hope to possess or control, can only aspire to meet, greet, encounter. That's when I felt it, a primal need to populate those mysterious waves with beings divine or demonic, and like the surf so sibilant at my feet, half-remembered legends lapped the edges of my mind.

Later, I perched atop a wild spume of silvering driftwood. Amidst a flurry of scricks and clicks, a tern had coaxed its fledgling to a piling just off shore. She would skim the glistening ripples, swoop up, fall down straight as a plumb bob, disappear with a splash then reappear in an skyward zoom, fish secured in her beak. With a flurry of shrieks and screams, a young girl ran to, then from, to and from, to and from the water where it shimmied onto sand. Her father grabbed her, hoisted her up onto his back; then, the mother took a snapshot of the pair. A white-haired couple plodded along, their white-haired dog racing ahead in a flurry of barks and yips, chasing a lone, white gull.

Zest of Chesapeake, above, and below? From my sea-sculpted seat I pictured some of the bay's more exotic denizens. The exuberant bristles and paddle-shaped feet of the clam worm. The prickly bumps of starfish skeleton, poking out through the skin of radiant starfish arms. And, needing neither witch rider nor seaweed reins, our very own *hippocampus erectus*, the lined seahorse.

Could a more improbable creature be imagined? A horse's head, a kangaroo's pouch, a fish's fins, a lizard's eyes, a dinosaur's bony plates, a monkey's prehensile tail, a chameleon's wardrobe and wafting, skin-like appendages that imitate algae to fool predators. They have no teeth, no stomach, and scarf up four thousand brine shrimp a day. Seahorses mate for life, and only males get pregnant. Every morning of their wedded life, the blissful couple greets each other by linking tails, twirling around, changing colors, then dancing off in opposite directions.

A friend just gave me a magazine that is celebrating the beginning of summer by offering a guide to the pleasures of the season. I looked the word up in the dictionary. 'Pleasure' means 'the enjoyment of what is good,' and I thought, wow, those seahorses are onto something. How about getting up every morning and meeting the day with a zestful swirl, a colorful, impassioned twirl? We are, after all, improbable creatures, spirits wed to clay, divine sparks flung on the wood of this world in hopes of a fine, bright conflagration, or maybe it's a joyous dance our maker had in mind?

As I left the beach yesterday, a pair of swans alighted on the tidal pool. Partners for life, they say, although sometimes swans cheat, reneging on their commitment to each other. I said a little prayer to bolster my own commitment to fishing terns and shrieking children, old folks, dogs, gulls. Light playing tag with the sparkling water. Waves laughing themselves onto shore. All the sweet and yes, the sour this day, this life shall offer. We are very, very good together.

The Comfort of Green

If you could just suspend your disbelief for a moment. Dismiss your need for empirical evidence. Imagine with me that, behind its closed and virgin eyelids, the unborn child sees green. Green the jungle waters of the amniotic sac, the enfolding darkness, the warm, protected tides. Green the silence, all passion and strife muffled, far away. Green the growing in that nine-month cushioned ride.

Do I exaggerate? Maybe, but scientifically speaking, green is life. Consider those two Greek words, *chloros*, green and *phyllon*, leaf. Chlorophyll is the molecule that uses the energy of sunlight to make carbohydrates from CO_2 and water. It absorbs well in the blue and red but poorly in the green portions of the spectrum, which is why tissue containing the molecule appears green. Green is our very breath, the primal exchange from which our planet evolved: carbon dioxide for oxygen, light for food.

I am mesmerized by green, now that I'm living in Chesapeake Country after a lifetime away. Thirty years in the concrete wilderness of Manhattan. Five on the vast gray mesas of northern New Mexico. Forgive my hyperbole, but as I drive down the street I am convinced that the woods are unable to contain their joy at my arrival. See how they run right down to the edge of the pavement, to gather me into their arms?

Back in New Mexico, people prided themselves on their love for the austere beauty of the high desert. "I had to go east to see my mother," someone might say. "There was all that *broccoli*." And everyone would laugh knowingly. As if disdain could compensate for what we lacked: the consoling, companioning presence of things green and growing.

I walk down any road, enchanted. Green is a riotous abundance, an effervescence spilling forth, a verdant champagne. I see birds on lawns, telephone poles, I hear them chirp or twitter. But when they disappear into the exuberant mass of trees, they become something else: the green beak of the living world, piping its very own song.

Green beckons, like a crooked finger. Seduces, like a whispered secret. I sit on my friend's deck, staring intently into the woods that surround her house. Inside that luxurious flourishing I detect a pale emerald glow. Magic? Yes, but thoroughly explicable. Plant pigments accept all other colors but reject green, which then builds up a kind of spectral surplus that transfuses what light remains. Botanists call it "the green window." I prefer to think that the sun threads her darting needles with green to stitch us all together. Trees, bushes, birds, people … we are all one fabric, one whole and arboreal cloth. What to do when the scissors go snip, snip, snip?

When I found my new house, I rejoiced, for behind me lay a thick expanse of trees. I moved in on a Monday, set up my back bedroom office to green applause. On Friday, I swear, just four days later, I stumbled sleepily into my office to see what all the noise was about. Outside I saw a vacant brown lot dotted with mammoth bonfires. Bulldozers roved among the burning piles like grazing dinosaurs. The herbaceous monsters had devoured my woods, quite literally, overnight. There's a road back there now, an inert ribbon of cement, and soon more people will come, I have counted hookups for at least a dozen houses. The people will eat and drink, work and play, but where will be the comfort of green? Farther and farther away, I suppose. And if the story of my homecoming repeats itself – as it will – I fear we are very busy sending ourselves into exile.

No conclusions here. From the green heart of the growing world a green pulse continues to throb. I know what it's like, to be cut loose from that umbilical cord, so I just hope we can all stay connected to it for as long as we inhabit this womb called Earth.

Barnacles and Tides

Beyond the gasp of white sails rounding the bend, or white clouds drifting on a pale blue sky. Below the river's sparkling, corrugated surface, where dragonflies and seagulls chase the waves. Under the water, that's where you would find me most summer days in childhood. Sipping from my china cup at mermaid tea parties. Or watching barnacles.

Down there, everything was different. Land's crisp outlines gave way to a green-tinged, myopic blur. Floating with the current, my long hair twined around my arms like seaweed. The cantankerous buzz of boat motors mellowed. The percussive beat of waves on sand softened. And the thick white crust on our pier pilings blossomed into a garden of living flowers.

I could hold my breath well over a minute. Plenty of time to submerge next to a post and watch the pointy little beaks inside each hexagonal shell open. A delicate hand would emerge then. Spread feathery fingers. Wave them back and forth in a slow, languid arc. To and fro, a serene pendulum. From one side, tranquil, to the other side, hypnotic. If, breaking the spell, I would raise one of my own fingers and bring it up close, quicker than quick, all the tiny doors on all the tiny houses would close up tight. Then one by one, the mysterious inhabitants would come out again.

It was a magic show meant for me alone. A delightful game I could enjoy 60 seconds at a time. And when, last week, I sat down to write about tides, this memory washed up like driftwood. A little research revealed the connection, for barnacles are creatures of the tidal pool, that place where land and water meet for conversation two times each day. The waving fingers I remember are actually legs. They sweep plankton from the water into the creature's mouth which, along with its stomach and sex organs, is buried inside six fixed and four moveable plates.

Every barnacle is both male and female. One will send out a long tubular penis into another, which broods the fertilized eggs then releases over 10,000 larvae. These swim freely for many days, eventually finding their way to the upper zone of some new pool. Using cement glands, the larvae attach themselves to a smooth surface where water only comes in at high tide: pier post, boat, rock. On that spot they construct calcium carbonate houses with doors that can open to feed or close up tight to seal in water during long hours of drought.

The tide itself is a kind of door that swings on gravity's rusty hinge. Yanked open by sun and moon. Slammed shut by Earth herself. Vast energies swirl around us, and we can steep ourselves in those cosmic rhythms. The rising and falling of water. Earth's chest heaving up and down, her breath flowing in and out. The Chesapeake's length makes it unique among estuaries, for when one high tide reaches the head of the bay near Havre de Grace, the next high tide is just entering near the Bridge Tunnel.

It belongs to all of us, this music, no matter where we live. This bass and treble. These notes eternally shifting into new arrangements of high and low, wet and dry, salt and fresh. I think of other alternating rhythms: silence and speech. Action and rest. Love and fear. The light that brings us life is a tide, swelling and emptying from solstice to solstice. Hunger is a tide that peaks and ebbs, and we are creatures of many and various hungers. Forward and back. Near and far. Exposed and hidden. Reliable, the ocean's restless creeping, but other movements: not so predictable.

I'm not certain how much we can learn from the barnacle, a creature with no heart or brain. Still, there it is: equanimity in the face of constant change.

The Gift

The grass on the path is still wet with dew, still fondled by the pure and virgin morning, still shimmering in its pristine, inviolate genesis. I walk amidst a profusion of butterflies, ripening berries and fat white mushrooms, under trees that loom like legendary beasts. The thick air throbs with the desiccated hum of locusts, crickets, grasshoppers, cicadas, a pandemonium pulse that inflates to crescendo then deflates to silence for mysterious reasons known only to itself.

I push aside a thick, leafy curtain to emerge onto the naked apron of sand. Is that applause? Or is it harpsichord notes of light flashing on water's keyboard? I'm not sure, but I'm urged forward, to where the waves stack up in silken tiers on the shore, a tender and refulgent caress my skin yearns for, so I slip out of my sandals and into the river's spectral green realm.

Stiff, awkward grasses become pliant and graceful. Minnows dart around my feet, tickling my toes. Emboldened, I wade deeper. Every step sends out concentric sunbright circles from the stone of me dropped into this moment, this moment, this moment, until I stand motionless in the fragile breeze.

I imagine I am some long-legged bird, some shore-hugging creature unsuited to the open blue water where the albatross flies or the whales sing, no, I prefer my amphibian walk, neither of the land nor of the sea but of both. Like the great blue heron I am a solitary predator, hunting alone. Unlike the heron, I might not recognize nourishment when it appears, a thought that propels me to continue my aqueous amble parallel to the beach, looking for I know not what.

Could it be the feel of mud, so silky soft underfoot? The surprise when a startled crab scuttles away? Maybe it's the way the water swirls warm then cold then warm again that beckons me on. I can't name the object of my quest, yet, as I reach the narrow channel into a tidal pool I am excited, expectant. It might be just there, just around that curve, where the tide hurries inward, where floating leaves rush by on their secret and urgent mission, that I might come face to face with something hitherto submerged, hidden, undiscovered.

My friend's daughter will soon be married. Lela and Joel will push aside the thick curtain of childhood to emerge together onto life's naked stage, and I've found here the perfect wedding gift. I'll send them the wisdom of the great blue heron, a creature that is gregarious during nesting season, but solitary and territorial during the rest of the year. They'll remember to keep their marriage an amphibian journey, never losing themselves completely in each other or in their children but always holding onto the submerged and undiscovered mystery that propels us, for reasons known only to ourselves, to seek expectantly for we know not what. I'm delivering their present just now, in person, arriving to surprise them on my great blue wings.

The Pier

These boards. Grayed from wind and water. Green-stained from moss and algae. White-streaked from bird droppings. Time-buffed to a rich patina. My bare feet want to linger here, flesh warmed by the sun-drenched wood, but memory scampers off to the sunshine of a distant day. When I watched my father build this pier plank by raw pine plank. Sweat glistened on his face. I sat on a freshly-split log stair, clutching a glass bottle of orange soda pop. Each of my endless questions received the same smothered response, for my father's mouth was filled with nails, but one question – What makes waves? – I can answer for myself today.

It walked with me through the trees, the wind, touching each leaf as we clambered down the hillside. I can go no further than this dock, but the wind continues on. Making for itself a moveable staircase of water and air molecules. Traveling across the creek, out into the river, through the bay, to the ocean. Clasping hands with other winds from far off lands. Dancing with giant currents that gyre and eddy around the globe in a planetary celebration of energy and motion that I don't have to budge one inch to join.

Through wooden slats I watch the water slide shoreward. Light splashes off its wavering surface and back onto the pier in a brightsome, undulating mosaic. Stirred by the soft salt breeze, tree limbs cast quivering shadows on cliff and creek, while above me, white clouds roil with gray as they drift across their own blue sea. Seagulls, ospreys, crows. Dragonflies, butterflies, wasps. The air is aslant with wings and tangled with sound: warbles, trills, whistles; the slap of fish falling back from their sunward leaps; and always, the liquid tattoo of waves on sand.

My trusty online encyclopedia tells me that, in physics, motion means a change in the position of a body with respect to time, as measured by a particular observer in a specific frame of reference. Memory records such changes, yes? I remember childhood, when the pier and I were not so weathered. The pier, too, remembers: its worn metal cleats still wait for boats that have long since been junked; frayed rope from abandoned crab traps still clings to its pilings.

And the beach remembers. This morning I saw 'coon tracks in the sand. The faint tracings of a meandering periwinkle. The short squat imprint of a twig that rested briefly then ran away with the wind. Every passing wave leaves its inky autograph: pebbles, bits of shell, leaf mold. The swash pushes sediment in at an angle; the backwash pulls it out perpendicular to the shore, hence, that zigzag footprint called beach drift. The pebbles remember themselves in larger incarnations: rocks, boulders, mountains. The shells remember their fleshy occupants. Since all life on Earth began in the sea, the sea itself – that particular observer, that specific frame of reference – surely the sea remembers us?

When I was a young girl this creek froze over every winter. All the kids in the neighborhood ice-skated around our pier. Laughter rang from hill to hill, shore to shore. Games of tag. Show-off stunts. The flash of moonlight on silver skate blades. Hot chocolate in my father's thermos. But the creek hasn't frozen over in years. Those giant currents are warming us into a future substantially different from the past, as just about any observer can measure.

Memory scampers off to the sunshine of a distant day. 65 million, 250 million, 488 million years ago. Planetary gyres and eddies, the great extinction events that changed evolutionary history. And now, something new in this cosmic celebration: the energy and motion of human awareness.

Over raised dots of sunlight, water's blind fingers play lightly. Flung against the sky, passing birds make an *I Ching* of lines long and short. The whole planet is groping. Stumbling as one towards something only we humans can imagine or create. We are not fallen leaves, floating helplessly to shore like shipwrecked boats, we can plot another course, arrive somewhere else, think up new names for a world no one has ever known before. Ours.

The Zone[*]

When I walk the beach – and I walk the beach every day, now that summer's here – when I tramp or traipse or amble or ramble along the shore. And the breaking waves are a white lace flounce edging the sand. And the breaking waves are a salty pulse coursing steady in the sand. Earth's heartbeat and my own wed together on the sand. In the splashing water I'm walking, looking down.

They call it the swash zone. Uprush meets backwash, inflow meets rundown, water's mantra of longing meets her sigh of satisfaction. Here is where dizzy collides with giddy, intoxication confronts delirium, I can lose myself in the place that's neither in nor out but in and out at the same moment and hence, just beyond the reach of space and time.

Here is where you find them, on the pristine, virgin sand: old logs and wet shells being ground to slivers and glints. Flutes of driftwood, holes bored out by tiny creatures, and by time. Castles don't last long here, nor can footprints endure. And if you stop. If you halt your forward motion. If, standing straight as an arrow, you try to remain still as a rock, the sand will melt from under, mound up over, your feet. You'll sink deep, deeper, you'll begin to think you're rooted, that you belong here, but the tether is misleading and the mooring false. Your real home is constant motion. Now you must go on.

All a-swell the light has been, these past weeks. Every morning, an earlier dawn. Every evening, a later dusk. Every day, a waxing radiance, an almost unbearable fullness, like a woman in her ninth month. This year, at precisely 18:06 Greenwich Mean, the sun will be tethered straight as an arrow, still as a rock, directly above the outermost boundary of the tropics, the parallel of latitude which is 23.5 degrees north of the equator.

---

[*] Author's note. This was published on June 21, 2007; hence, the time and date references.

This day is our longest, this night our shortest. By tomorrow, our star's moorings will already have loosened. The sun will be one tick further south, our day one tock shorter. We're living in the swash zone now. The uprushing, inflowing, breaking wave of light has collided with light's backwash. Summer has just given birth.

Once upon a time, they lit bonfires on Midsummer's Eve. They danced and drank and sang, as if to match the sky's delirium with their own intoxication. Magic ruled, and midsummer night dreams. Children twined flowers around the horns of bulls. Young girls scryed for future husbands. Lovers leapt through flames then bedded in the bushes. Healers plucked their most potent herbs. The people prayed and partied for what the people wanted: health and wealth and fertile fields, fecund beasts, plenty of kids.

That was then. Now we're living in the swash zone. The backwash of our past desires has collided with the uprushing, inflowing, breaking wave of our future needs. Humanity tramps and traipses, ambles and rambles along a giddy edge, a dizzy brink. We cannot stop, we cannot halt our forward motion, we must move on down the pristine, virgin shore. Where every passing day casts up new questions. Grinds old answers down to slivers and glints.

Last week, as I left the beach, I passed a woman carrying her toddler back to the parking lot. "She's afraid of sand," the tired mother said to me, and I thought, Aren't we all? I mean, who doesn't want to run from a place where the selvage is unraveling?

Yet here it is, the summer solstice. And here we are, brothers and sisters birthed together in a newborn season, ready to pray and party for what we're ready to want, our outmoded longings washing out, our newer satisfactions swashing in, a hazy crazy maybe zone, a midsummer night's dream.

Sea Nettles

The summer solstice has come and gone, but the sea nettles are here to stay. I stand on the pier looking down into the bottle green depths of the Patuxent. The sun has burnished the air into a metallic amalgam of smells: wood, salt water, exposed barnacles, sea weed. Insects hum, a chorus that rises and falls, ebbs and flows like the waves. How wonderful it would be to dive off this hot pier into the cool water. How delightful, to leave behind the friction of every day living for a skin of liquid velvet. I could kick my way free of all worries. Back to the bliss of the womb, perhaps. Or even further. To some mindless, amphibian state.

Automatically, with the reflexes of a child raised on this river, I start to count the nettles. There are only a few on the surface, but moment by moment more ghostly shapes arise from nether darkness into the light, like eerie, diaphanous negatives developing in a chemical bath. I give up counting: they are as numberless as the stars. Their umbrella shaped heads pump rhythmically with the current, and their long tentacles trail behind them in an entrancing, balletic display. That otherworldly grace belies the venomous reality of those delicate threads. Poison enough to paralyze a small fish. Deliver a sharp sting and red welts to human flesh. If I scooped one up in a crab net, it would collapse instantly into an inert mass of brainless, heartless, boneless jelly. Removed from the water which comprises 98% of its being, the creature would dry up quickly, expiring into its trace elements of salt and protein with a faint stink.

I recall summer days long past, when this pier was a blur of children – cousins, neighbors, friends. A medley of legs and arms and laughter. Bare skin, wet bathing suits. A background drone of outboard motors near and far. While the adults were off somewhere doing whatever adults do, we swam, most of us, while some stood guard, furiously scooping up sea nettles in crab nets then running to dump them on shore. At regular intervals, pained cries: "I've been stung!" Or, "One got me!" Or just a wordless shriek and a churn of water as the victim rushed to shore for the placebo comfort of sand rubbed on burning skin. And after, a chance to exact revenge by taking up sentry duty, with upright net pole and vigilant eyes.

Yet we swam. I remember diving headlong off this very pier piling, eyes closed tightly, hoping to complete my underwater arc unscathed but braced for the awful instant of entanglement, when naked flesh would burst upon a jumble of slithering tentacles. I would fight my way to the surface then, pawing to rid face or neck of the adhesive, gelatinous fire.

We strapped on water skis despite the virtual certainty of getting stung while waiting for the boat to pick us up. When one of us would be put to bed with a thick paste of baking soda applied to a swollen body part, the rest of us went right on. Cavorted and splashed. Played mermaid or seahorse or water basketball, all in a gloriously adult-free zone, because grown ups were scairdy cats, afraid to take their pleasure for fear of a little pain. And I'm one of them. Too chicken to swim in this water now that the nettles are back. I understand they're particularly fond of the Chesapeake Bay, where the right mix of salt and fresh makes the water brackish, their preferred environment.

Life itself is pretty brackish. Pretty much a mix of salt and fresh. Pain of one sort or another is continually arising from the nether darkness. The dangers are as numberless as the stars. But the next time I'm tempted to hold back on living because of some possible hurt, I'm going to consult with the child I was. I think I already know what she's going to say.

Woodswalk

Where I was is not where I am. That grassy, sunbright meadow. This dark shroud of trees. That smiling froth of birdsong. This somber silence. Purposeful, expansive strides brought me here. Now, my feet make hesitant progress on a narrow ribbon of path that curls and furls as it will, not as I plan.

I pause. My breath slows to match the dark and secret pulse of sap. I remember high school botany class. Water and inorganic nutrients, tugged from the soil through the roots and up along the inert xylem cells. The magic of photosynthesis. Presto-change-o, abrakazam, now the water carries sugar into the living phloem cells. Down, around, throughout. Yes. I remember. How to breathe. Taking in air's rich elixir. Letting it steep in lung sac, bone marrow. Down core of heart, pith of soul, then through and out.

Pausing winds down to stopping. I sit on a moss-clad log, letting my body adjust to the stillness. Like when you walk into a dark room. The time it takes for your eyes to adapt is the measure of the brightness you left behind, and I've left behind a lot of churning. A lot of plans and schemes. A whole big enterprise that sometimes seems more an industry I have to support than a life I get to live.

As quiescent hush silences militant maelstrom, I am free to be here, only here, in the midst of this vertical embrace, this upright hug, this skyward clasp of trees thrusting up, up, up – I see them – of roots plunging down, down, down – I don't see them, but sense their blind groping into enigmatic depths. I can't see my own roots, either, but with the rising, falling flow of sapwater everywhere around, I imagine that the tiny hairs all along my arms and legs can become, presto-change-o, abrakazam, fine long tendrils growing me down into the earth. Finding me nourishment, and a strong anchor.

Still at last, I can at last take notice. High above, sunlight trembles onto every leaf fluttering in the wind. Here below, leafshadows wobble and jog, shudder and shake, a spotted dotted leafsong, a stippled spangled leafdance, a freckled flash of leaf-fingers playing the keyboard that is me, releasing from my heart a splash of leafnotes, presto-change-o, abrakazam, I am music, I am dance. My face now sports a leafsmile, and my soul claps leafhands in wonder and delight.

I rise, slowly, not wanting to break the spell. The path that had seemed so cantankerous and confused is now a loopy, meandering marvel. I guess it really is like Dante said. When he found his way to paradise. Because he let himself awaken "in a dark wood/Where the straight way was lost." I shudder to think how many paradises I have forfeited in my lifetime, and tomorrow, when I pick up the paper to read the news, I'll remember today's walk in a dark woods. I'll remember to remind myself, presto-change-o, abrakazam, we're all just waking up.

BLUE CRAB ETUDE

Nana taught me how. No matter how early I got up or how fast I slipped on my summer uniform of shorts, top and flip-flops, she would already be down there in her sundress and hat. Kneeling on the rough wood planks of the dock. Chest butted up against a piling. Left hand working the string, right hand holding the net.

I see the scene so clearly. Those four, front-most pier posts, darkly creosoted, each wrapped with pale twine. The cord plays out into the water at a wide angle to its tether on the piling, and no child of the river needs to be told what invisible tug o' war holds the line so taut. On the sandy creek bottom, a blue crab struggles to swim away with its carrion prize: a chicken neck tied tightly to the end of the string my grandmother painstakingly works.

On memory's split screen, I see a close-up of her left hand: the twine, threaded through Nana's fore and middle fingers, pinned in place with her thumb. Over and under. Thumb up, thumb down. Inch by upward bound inch, crab and bait rise. Where it slices into the water, the net pole appears to break, a distortion that makes distance hard to gauge. Speed is out of the question, the water offers too much resistance, so with a stiff right arm, Nana maneuvers the net's wooden shaft by quark-sized increments until the head is directly under the feeding, oblivious creature. Anything, even a flickering shadow, will startle her prey into its peculiar, sideways scuttle. She continues. Cautiously. To tease that awkward trio – crab, baited string and meshed hoop – to the surface. Then one deft, skyward jerk. "Got him," she says, grinning. I scamper off to the live-box with our catch.

Popi also taught me how, although kids were not welcome to join him. "You're too noisy," he would bark, "You scare the crabs away." So I would watch from a distance as he waded along the shore like some long-legged marsh bird. Pant legs rolled up above bony knees. Skinny calves protruding. His far off, silent prowling is keyed forever, in my mind, to the constant slap of water against pier pilings, against moored boats, against the endless beach where tall sea grass whispers *snick snick* in a hot, dry breeze.

Popi is a vigilant hunter. He marches all day from one end of our cove to the other, net pole cradled – shotgun style – against a bent left elbow. From that position he can brandish either end of his weapon. Wield the wooden handle to poke under logs and rocks. Or, like a bayonet, stab the hoop end into the water to nab his elusive prey: a blue crab, freshly molted, butter soft. Supremely confident in his ability, Popi refuses to carry with him any sissy storage basket. Instead, he returns to the pier with two or three huge jimmies stacked in the same net he used for their capture. Popi's grin is all for himself. Tucked into his chin. Elusive.

An etude is a musical composition designed to provide practice in a particular technical skill on a solo instrument. Pianists may turn to Chopin to learn their parallel thirds. Flutists might rely on Boehm for their fingering style. I could walk down to the pier right now and catch a crab the way my grandparents showed me. Or I could stay at this desk. Teasing thoughts to the surface word by upward-bound word.

And what of this perpetual tug 'o war called life, where a taut line is sometimes all we have of what we need. Where bait and prize are often indistinguishable. And there's too much resistance. Too long a solitary prowl. I know that ceaseless effort is the cost of all things hoped for, yet ever and always I am tempted by the hiss of *What's the use?* Still, I don't give up. Nana and Popi didn't teach me how.

Butterfly Q & A

And when she asked me, "What name should I give to these flowers? Yellow and white? Sun and moon? Ivory and molten gold?" I replied, "That's silly. It's just honeysuckle."

And when she asked me, "What name should I give to this scent? A perfume? An intoxication? Perfect bliss?" I replied, "That's silly. It's just honeysuckle."

But she would neither be silenced nor dismissed. "What hunger does this nectar satisfy?" she probed, and I remembered. A little girl in plaid shorts and pigtails. A small fist clutching a broken branch: leaves like the emerald tongues of panting fairy dogs. Flowers white as ivory moons, yellow as melting sunshine. Burying my nose in blossoms. In a whirling, swirling, reeling, spinning universe of sweet, of good, of happy. Besotted with it. Addled with it. Then the wondrous anticipation of a further, an attainable, an ineluctable joy: one pinch on a pale green stopper. The triumphal tug. The ambrosial droplet.

"What hunger does this nectar satisfy?" she repeated, and I thought hard. It wasn't that the pleasure was forbidden – my father had showed me how, after all. Once. Twice. Then he forgot. Moved on to what he thought was more important business, the weighty worries of his grownup world. But I foraged at the edge of the woods, tippling honeysuckle, a task vastly superior to any my father might accomplish. Even then I knew what really mattered, with a conviction as sure and delicious as the liquor I imbibed.

Carl Linnaeus gave honeysuckle its botanical genus, *lonicera*. Carl Linnaeus also called the butterfly the *imago*, Latin for 'image' or 'likeness.' It's not the stubborn, taciturn egg nor the voracious caterpillar nor the shrewd and secretive pupa hidden in its silky cocoon that defines what the adult of the species can aspire to, no. It's a high-flying, free-wheeling, winged beauty that is the image and likeness of the creature's mature form.

Now she wants to move on to another subject, demanding to know what holiday we Americans celebrate in the month of July. When I say, "Independence Day," she asks, "What does this mean?" I glibly respond, "Freedom," thinking she'll be satisfied, but no, she is repeating her earlier question, "What hunger does this nectar satisfy?"

I'm stumped. I've never thought of freedom as a food, but then, I've been grown up for so long I've forgotten what the adult of the human species should aspire to. I've mistaken stubborn, voracious and shrewd for mature, disregarding the high-flying, free-wheeling beauty in whose image and likeness we were made. It's a whirling, swirling universe of sweet, of good, of happy, after all, and I'm wondering if what we've been calling the American Dream all this time is now a silky, too-tight cocoon?

Only a question. Maybe I'll ask her about it, if she ever comes back. I hope she hasn't decided she has more important things to do, because if she laughs and says, "That's silly," I'll be really upset.

Berries, Blossoms, Bunting

So I walk the shore, picking up fragments of my scattered self – a feather, a shell, a knobbly piece of driftwood. Earth, sea, sky. The tri-weave basket that holds us all. Three strands braided to bind us. A trinity indwelling anyone dwelling on this planet.

At least, I think this explains it. Why I snatch at each object as if it were some crucial clue in a mystery I must solve. A wave-scrubbed shell; a cast-off feather; a useless chard of wood; a solitary, beach-combing woman – nithings in a vast universe, all, and yet each flames forth with a singular and urgent beauty.

At least, I think this explains it. Why it pleases me to see my own sandy footprints mixed in with the tattered hieroglyphs of bird tracks. Why I cried, yesterday, over the turtle which had wandered into my minuscule back yard. There, he'd be safe, but have no ready access to food and water, so I let him go in the thin strip of woods behind my house. There, he'd be free to seek what he needs to live, but his life would be in constant peril from the steady stream of cars into a nearby parking lot. There were no good choices left for that turtle.

At least, I think this explains it. Why it bothered me so much when the flags and bunting for July 4th went up in Walmart right after Memorial Day, and as soon as the Independence Day weekend passes, back-to-school items will appear along with clearance sales and fall clothes. Summer, it seems, is one month long now. We're more firmly tethered to marketing cycles than to Nature's cycle of seasons.

At least, I think this explains it. Why I've been keeping such a vigilant watch on those blackberry bushes. The shy green blush. The profligate cascades of flowers. The brown tatters of petals clinging to a tight green knob. Then a rust-colored blush, a pristine virgin red, a ripe black purpled with juice and promise. I'll stay sentinel throughout the coming months. Walmart will be decorated for Christmas when emerald leaves turn topaz and birds finish off those berries. Just as the naked stems settle into their snow-blanketed beds, Walmart will be urging us to buy next spring's fashions.

And that explains it. Why most of us teeter through life unbalanced, on edge, anxious, like overworked donkeys chasing carrots-on-sticks. Forget the tri-weave basket of earth, sea and sky that contains us in a slow, unfolding now. Packaging, marketing and sales, that's the braid that binds us fast to an uneasy if, then, when.

On July 4, 1776, the 13 colonies declared their independence from an oppressive regime that impinged on "life, liberty and the pursuit of happiness." That was freedom's first flowering, like the cascades of springtime blossoms on blackberry bushes. Our understanding of freedom has ripened over the years: slavery is wrong, stealing land from indigenous people is wrong. One day we'll be able to pluck freedom's sweet, sustaining fruit: war itself is wrong. Meanwhile, we need to declare our independence from an oppressive regime of commercialization that has us wandering around like that turtle I found yesterday. To provide for ourselves by destroying our connection to the natural world is no good choice at all.

So here, take my osprey feather. Its shaft is called a rachis. Fused to that are branches called barbs, but you don't need to know that to call my feather beautiful, its graceful arc all mottled brown and white.

Take my oyster shell. It could be washed up from Miocene era sediment, some 20 million years old. You'll love its gleaming patina: cameo pink, dove gray, lucent copper. And the way it curves so perfectly into the palm of your hand, you'll enjoy that, as well.

Take my long, thin, crooked stick of driftwood, sanded smooth as silk by the bay. Salt and time have stained its grain into ink-dark, wave-like whorls. It would be easy to fall into those eddying depths, don't you think?

Take all my little trinkets; you'll need them. As we walk time's wave-lapped shore, picking up remnants of our scattered Self.

The Gathering

Plucking apples one by one, to make cider in the wooden press. Above a leafy green fretwork, the ripening moon hangs in a late afternoon sky. A mockingbird scolds from its rooftop perch, and in the garden, fat bees trundle from one blossom to the next, collecting nectar to make honey in their secret, mysterious press. If I had wings, I, too, could drone contentedly about my task, but these two arms will have to do, so I hum softly to myself. It feels good to be nestled within earth's two great wings of morning and evening, a day much like all the others yet unique unto itself, simultaneously unremarkable and unrepeatable.

With my friends away, their homestead is my responsibility these next few hours. In the barn, I trade a five gallon bucket filled with apples for a stack of empty, half-pint berry boxes, and stop to watch the swallows flit from beam to beam in endless pursuit of their insect meal. My trek back to the garden is enlivened by the darting shimmer of dragonflies, also hunting insect prey, and I remember a story I read once, long ago, about dragonflies, those harbingers of change. Born of water, maturing into air, living their short, magical lives with an exuberant joy we might all do well to imitate in our own ephemeral existence.

The blackberries are heavy with sunshine. They smell purple, they taste purple, they stain my fingers purple, and tomorrow, someone will buy them at the store and take this sweet purple sunshine home to eat. I pray that their meal will somehow include the lacy filigree of blackberry leaves, gold-stippled in this early evening light. And the eager squash vines hauling themselves upwards on the fruit-laden arc of blackberry branches bending to touch the earth. And the elegiac cooing of the doves. And the cloud-scarves draped so elegantly across sky's azure shoulders, gauzy wisps of white, of pink, of lavender, of gray.

Yes, evening is coming on now. The sheep are bleating in the field, crowded together by the gate which I'll unlatch so they can rush into the warm arms of the waiting barn. I'll round up the chickens, and herd the turkeys into their roosts. Soft clucks and muted gobbles will form the words of this night's lullaby, set to the pleated pulsing of crickets and frogs, punctuated by the haphazard strobe of fireflies, as darkness settles on the homestead like a broody hen's extended wing.

My friend, the homesteader, will rise before dawn tomorrow, to lead the sheep out, to let the chickens and turkeys run free, and I shall, no doubt, be dreaming still as I dart about on wings that blossom from azure shoulders, feathers all pink and white and lavender and gray, gathering a sweet and secret nectar from each and every task. And who's to say it isn't real food, real drink? Who would dare to call it merely magical, this meal? This joyful, this ephemeral, this sacred, this unremarkable, unrepeatable day.

Mimosa Moment

The blooms made me stop, the scent made me linger, the buds made me wonder about almost everything.

I know, I know, it isn't fair. You're already asking, Who, what, where? When, how, why?

Let's start over.

It was sometime in July. All the roads were lined with effervescence of mimosa. Flowers like fans, ballerinas, balloons, butterflies, I couldn't help myself, I had to get up close to one, so I parked my car on a grassy knoll, scrambled over a ditch, up a hill, into a whorl of scent as delicate as pink cobwebs, as fragile as blushing soap bubbles, I thought, How is it I have lived so long burdened by gravity when all along a nirvana of weightlessness has been waiting for me, disguised as a simple perfume?

I plucked one gossamer blossom. Tickled my cheek into a fuzzy giggle with it. Painted the flesh of one arm incandescent with a fairy brush of it. I couldn't fathom how something so small and gentle could grip my heart like a strong fist. Could make me want to pitch a tent. Spend the rest of my life there, a devotee of Mimosa.

I would sleep at night on green feathers, under a blanket soft as sunrise. Every morning I would wake, ready to go out and preach Mimosa to our harsh, our strident, our dog-eat-dog, survival-of-the-fittest, looking-out-for-number-one world. Billions of people would convert to Mimosa, coining new phrases for old values like tenderness and compassion. We would abandon force as a path to change and learn the power of cooperation, but as I stepped up to the podium to accept my Nobel Peace Prize, a bumblebee landed on an eye-level branch, and that's when I noticed the buds.

Tight green knobs, impenetrable verdigris knots, solid, infrangible nodes from which nothing could emerge and yet, from each hard pebble an effusion of soft threads had burst. A silky, extravagant testament to the unlikely. As astonishing a witness to surprising potential as pink cobwebs of morning spun from the black silk of night.

That was July, this is August. Just passing, the season for mimosa, and just passing, a woman I know, who would have become a dear friend except the impenetrable knot of sickness claimed her first. The last time I saw her, she lay in bed stroking her cat's white fur with fingers thin as twigs. The trees beyond her bedroom window seemed to reach in and stroke us both, a peaceful, consoling moment, and although she is leaving behind the pebble of her body, I know her soul will blossom into a surprise of potential.

Religion wants to teach us there is life after death. Wants to teach us tenderness and compassion as well. Most of us seem not to have learned those lessons, so maybe after all we should all convert to Mimosa, which proclaims what it also proves: that just beyond the hard, tight bud of the present, an extravagant and improbable future awaits. Amen.

Secrets of Loveliness

When I was a teenager, I had a book called *Secrets of Loveliness*. Its back cover promised tips to transform awkward girls into feminine beauties. I remember diligently poring over every chapter, convinced there was, indeed, some secret, the discovery of which would magically propel me beyond confused adolescence into the stable form haywire hormones suggested I might one day become.

Evolution – in one person's life or in the life of an entire species – is a tricky thing. I've heard that the horse and the bison once had a common ancestor. When faced with danger, some members of the now-extinct hipparianon species chose to run, developing the horse's long legs, and muscles appropriate to speed. Other hipparionons chose to stand and fight the threat, developing the bison's bulk, and muscles appropriate to charging. Their different response patterns dictated divergent evolutionary outcomes for these creatures.

This summer, on a pilgrimage to North Carolina's Grandfather Mountain, I think I may have heard the human gene pool split. I was walking the mile-high swinging bridge with a handful of other tourists. We all paused, looking down to where a hawk spiraled lazily on air currents. To where clouds shrouded thin ribbons of highway spooling out in all directions 5,000 feet below. "I could stay up here a while," a boy behind me sighed to his companion, his voice trailing off in ecstatic communion with Nature's grandeur. Then his voice hardened. "I could stay up here an hour." As if, between breaths, from one heartbeat to the next, he had glimpsed an unbearable spaciousness on which he had to impose an arbitrary time limit.

I believe that the secret to humanity's becoming is buried in the book each of us writes as a response to Nature. Some of us can acknowledge we are part of a larger whole. We are comfortable with mystery, Nature's enigmatic presence comforts us, we're willing to allow the ebb and flow of the non-human world to imprint itself on us, claim us for its own.

But some human beings seem unable to endure Nature's existential otherness. When I lived in New York City many years ago, I created a project for the children of Manhattan's Lower East Side, schlepping them up to Central Park, where they could write poetry and exercise the body-mind-spirit continuum. Instead of inspiring and delighting these kids, the park terrified them. They wouldn't sit on the grass, which was dirty, they said, yet they would gleefully cavort on the playground's grimy asphalt, chasing each other with dead, maggot-infested pigeons.

Marketing pundit Kevin O'Keefe points out in his book, *The Average American*, that the typical citizen believes Nature is sacred but spends 95% of his time indoors. It seems to me some human beings are set on remaining in their man-made comfort zone, like frightened children. What they will evolve into I can't foresee, but me, I think I'll take my chances with that other species, the one secretly but surely evolving into ecstatic communion with loveliness and grandeur.

SURRENDER TO SOLITUDE

Night's soft surround begins here, in the gloaming, with crickets and cicadas, vast tidal currents of sound that rise up to flood the tall green crowns of pines, then cascade down and out into thick green grass, carrying the safe contours and certain colors of day into mysterious darkness.

Soon the stars will out. I shall find them in the sky, of course, splayed and spangled, but if I look amidst the bristled, ebony pine boughs I shall find them, ripe cones of light, and if I look into the onyx river, I shall find them, submerged shells of light, and if, with some sixth or seventh sense I could look into the obscure pitch of my own heart, I should find stars there as well, incandescent, lamp-like, ready to hand should I choose to venture forth on whatever darksome path.

"And the light came from her body, and the night went through her grace," keens Leonard Cohen in his song, "Our Lady of Solitude." Devotion to the Virgin under that title began as a Holy Saturday observance, when the faithful entrusted to her the liminal hours between Good Friday's crucifixion and Easter Sunday's resurrection. In the 17th century, a donkey staggered into Oaxaca, Mexico and collapsed, dead. No one knew where it had come from, but when they examined his pack, they found a statue of Mary that wore a crown of diamonds and a black velvet robe. They built a church on the spot, and devotion to Our Lady of Solitude, patroness of mariners, is an integral part of Mexican spirituality to this day.

In the mid 1990s, I placed my own liminal hours in Mary's hands, leaving my cramped Manhattan apartment for a month-long retreat amidst the sand and saguro cactus of the Arizona desert surrounding Our Lady of Solitude House of Contemplative Prayer. Sr. Therese Sedlock, the founder, shared her eremitical lifestyle with a revolving community of seekers, each of us inhabiting one of four hermitages, the name of which, Sister explained, would symbolize the retreat's unique charism for its inhabitant. Mine was called *Adsum*, "Here I am," three words across which Abraham walked, plank-like, between the moment he heard God call his name and the moment he heard God's request. "Take your son, your only son, Isaac, whom you love...."

Here I am now, far from that desert in space and time. "Here I am," the crickets sing, echoing my thought. "Here I am," the quarter moon whispers, emerging from her hermitage of clouds. "Here I am," the jellyfish repeat, their presence announced not by sight or sound but by scent, a faint tang in the air most likely identifiable only to someone raised on this river, as I was. Scientists say there is no such thing as an objective observer. Reality is a participatory, interactive, relational event, since what we think of as matter is, at the quantum level, interconnected webs of energy, fields of possibility, waves of probability that ebb and flow as occasions, as events, as objects shaping each other in the very moment of encounter. Here I am, then, a concatenation of energies called crickets, called moon, called jellyfish, pier, river, woman, once solitary jewels, now, together, a glimmering crown to grace the night as she slips on her velvet black robe.

In the mauve light, I can just make out a heron perched on a nearby piling. All summer long she has fished these waters, skimming the surface as she flew from one secluded cove to another. In her throaty cry I hear Sr. Therese's words to me reverberate down the years. "If you were called to solitude, solitude would have sought you out." I had laughed at the time: abandoned at birth, an orphanage, my adopted father in his grave before my seventh birthday? Surely solitude had sought me out, skimming the surface of my life again and again as I sought for the absent primal bond, the missing family connection in religious community, in marriage, in myriad affiliations that seemed to promise communion yet always returned me to one secluded cove or another, where I would fish alone plagued by ambivalence toward the solitude I craved but also mistrusted. Is it truly God's call or just attachment disorder? Is it a yes unto greater life or a no to that pesky, uncontrollable human element?

My heron companion flies from her perch, flapping her two great and necessary wings. If there is only attraction and no repulsion, then the solitary is merely a misanthrope. If there is only allurement and no resistance, then the eremitical life is just a pleasure cruise. A vocation to solitude is a beckoning into the gloaming, that liminal state where safety and certainty fade into the soft surround. Our *adsum*, like Abraham's, comes after invitation, before sacrifice. We navigate uncharted depths, our patroness a woman who has stood in the ebb and flow of two energy fields. There we must stand as well, between crucifixion and resurrection, between memory and possibility, surrendering ourselves to the doubts that pound like nails, to the abyss of hours that gapes like an empty tomb.

In the dictionary, the primary legal definition of 'surrender' is 'to give up an estate to the person who has it in remainder, so as to merge it into a larger estate.' Such is the solitary's gift. Consider these fish that jump with exuberant abandon straight up into the air, slapping the water's still surface when they fall. Probability, deriving from past experience, says the fish are fleeing predators or chasing flies. But here I am in an empty moment, imagination fluttering like a shroud. What if, having all day watched winged shadows overhead, the fish are hurling themselves into the mauve air in hopes of achieving flight? What if the solitary consciousness, freed from memory's constricting grasp on the individual 'I am,' offers itself to the larger estate, the great and cosmic 'I am' which is even now hurling itself into a mauve future where the hard edges of separation fade into communion. Where light shines through the ink-black sky, the ebony trees, the onyx river, the pitch-dark obscurities of every human heart. Light like a lamp pouring forth from this body, this Christ, and the nights are as the days, flowing through this grace.

AUTUMN

Prequel to 'Autumn'

Outside? Pearl white clouds in a sapphire sky. Inside? A room full of women galumphing through our jazzercise routine in maladroit imitation of our agile teacher. We were executing some sequence, the name of which I never did catch, but: two steps to the right and forward. Twist, turn. Two steps to the left, back, twist, turn, meanwhile: arms extended at the shoulder, down, cross at the waist, up. Out, down, cross, up, out, down, then: from that dither of flopping legs and flapping arms I glance out the window to see: a single black crow streak upward into the lapis lazuli air.

Autumn, with its shifting winds and changing angle of light, seems to me to be the season that reminds us to celebrate the overarching sky, the encompassing air. Tomorrow, or the next day, or the next, whenever the river's surface is roughened by frills of whitecaps, I'll drive over to my favorite beach and watch the windsurfers. They will stand in waist-deep water, braving the increasing cold. They will manhandle stiff plastic sails into an upright position, then wait. Patiently. To catch that gust which will speed them along for an exhilarating moment they will share with the wind-borne gulls banking effortlessly overhead.

For me, the sky is shorthand for all that is beyond our reach or grasp. Unparalleled freedom. Inimitable grace. Earth is our home. The sea, well, eons ago, that was home, too, but the sky? It is the uncharted territory into which we long to fling ourselves, into which we cannot venture. Oh, sure, we have our airplanes and space shuttles, our satellites, our radar. We can track, we can trespass, but we can never belong, only awkwardly imitate that which does belong, by virtue of physiognomy or placement or ephemeral nature. I guess that's why I love to write about birds and butterflies, clouds and stars, light, sound, the scented air. I experience these as messengers that shuttle back and forth from where I am to where I might like to be, from what I am to what I might wish to become.

The sky is also a blue disguise for a black abyss, the empyrean heights, the vaulted heavens. Beyond what I see is a vastness that exceeds anything I can possibly imagine. Countless stars, each a sun for orbiting planets. Whirling concatenations of solar systems, swirling congregations of galaxies. The universe, they say, is 92 billion light years in diameter.

That number makes no sense to me, but it pleases me greatly to think that these reflections might pass on to you – from an infinite source – a tiny, tangible tingle. They begin with a meditation on the meaning of Labor Day, a holiday which, for many of us, marks the transition from summer to fall.

The Work We Do[*]

Today they call it Flag Ponds Nature Park, but yesterday – some 12 million years ago – it was an ocean where sharks hunted and whales met to give birth and yesterday – some fifty years ago – it was a Chesapeake Bay harbor where watermen fed their families by catching fish in pound-nets to sell in Baltimore and yesterday – just a week ago – it was a beach where a smattering of folk searched for fossils and yesterday – just 24 hours ago – two high tides brought new sand to the shore and tomorrow – maybe fifty years from now – today's beach will have turned into forest and tomorrow – maybe 12 million years from now – today's folk might have no language to describe what is here, or perhaps they'll call it ocean once again, or perhaps there will be nothing left but the silence from which it all emerged.

I think too much, I know that. While all those nice people combed the beach looking intently for black triangles fallen from the mouth of a Miocene-era shark, I sat morosely in my little chair just beyond the wrack line, staring at the debris the waves had ground, grated and pulverized into an homogeneous heap of white chips, black bits and gray smithereens. Somewhere in all that rubble a treasure could be found, but I could summon neither hope nor industry in the face of such an impossible task. I left.

On the path back to the parking lot, I stopped to read the signs. I especially loved the one about the edge effect. About the shifting boundaries between beach and dune, shrub and forest habitats. About the pioneer plants. The ones that can thrive in poor, sandy soil, reclaiming for land what belonged to the sea. Struggling with it, changing it, until other, less hardy vegetation can take root in the now fertile earth.

---

[*] Author's note. This was written in 2007. It is hoped that today's readers might be experiencing some of the new possibilities alluded to herein.

I noodled around at the Buoy Hotel, an old shanty left over from when the pound-net fishermen would camp out, February through November every year. Such hard labor. To cut and haul 50 foot poles from the forest. To hammer them into the harbor floor, 130 to support just one net. To trap the fish, scoop them into a boat, box them up for shipping. To mend the nets, keep the boats repaired, cook for themselves in cast iron skillets, make coffee in battered tin pots, drop into sleep on rough-hewn bunks under hand-made quilts, the day's work sweetened by dreams of hearth and home.

Back at the Visitor Center, I studied display cases filled with sand dollars, coral, leaf imprints, crocodile teeth, dolphin ear bones, sting ray dental plates, whale vertebrae, bones, petrified wood and Piscataway Indian fishing weights. Jumbled together without the neat labels, those precious artifacts would collapse into an homogenous heap of white chips, black bits and gray smithereens. I confess, it frightened me. If all my yesterdays are waves that grind and grate and pulverize. If this present moment is the wrack line. How will I ever know what to cherish, what to dismiss, what to keep, what to toss aside?

Labor Day is here already. It's supposed to be a tribute to the social and economic achievement of American workers. You know. The highest standard of living, the biggest gross national product, the best form of government; ours is a country of superlatives, okay, but 37 million Americans live below the poverty level, 47 million lack health insurance. It seems to me we're living in an era of shifting boundaries, with some new, some pioneer behaviors called for if we're to avoid the fate of those men who worked at the Buoy Hotel. Today, in a tree-framed pond, you can see the derelict pilings that yesterday had been their pier, before the sand bar took over, before the encroaching thrusts of spurge and thistle. The edge effect put an end to their labor, but ours is just beginning: a birthing of new possibilities this day so that dreams of hearth and home can endure unto tomorrow.

Knowing the Way by Water

The kayak is borrowed. I stop paddling almost as soon as I'm launched, studying the ragged edges of clouds as if they offered a map to the uncharted territory my life has become. I haven't called it home for over 40 years, but the instant I'm afloat, the molecules in my body want to align with the molecules of paddle, boat and water, reconstituting that concatenation of elements in a certain direction, towards a certain spot on a certain nearby creek where, on a certain bluff, a house once stood.

Last week's paper carried a story about a pod of whales beaching itself near the Cape of Good Hope. Hundreds of volunteers endured high winds and rough surf to try to push the creatures into open seas, but the whales kept swimming back to shore, and eventually the exhausted animals had to be shot, to prevent slow death by suffocation. No one understands such strandings. The whales could be sick, or following a confused leader, or attempting to rescue a stranded pod member sending off a distress call. Scientists think whales use magnetic fields and underwater topography to orient themselves, so a magnetic disturbance or peculiar coastline formation could bewilder them.

Now, I float amidst colored buoys and numbered channel markers, signs that mean something to someone but nothing to me. More significant is the cry of a baby osprey that scrapes the salty blue air near its twig-splayed nest. I recognize that familiar combination of morbid fear and importunate demand, and I'm tempted to turn my kayak towards the creek, the bluff, the collapsing house I keep wanting to call home, but the river's waters sparkle, and flow out to the bay, then out to the ocean, then out over the whole huge earth, so I follow the river, knowing this liquid is the united sparkling of two atoms of hydrogen and one atom of oxygen. Knowing each atom is the united sparkling of protons, neutrons, electrons. That each proton is the united sparkling of quarks and photons, each of which is a sparkling. Of. Something. That unites this kayak, this paddle, these hands that hold the paddle, the osprey's open beak, the twigs of its nest, those trees along the shore, this whole huge earth and, indeed, the universe itself. One united sparkling.

Home.

And if the old house is collapsing, I think that's a good thing. Like those whales, we've been sick, following confused leaders, attempting to rescue something that's beyond hope of repair. We all must contribute to the great work: finding a new orientation so we don't end up stranded on a deadly shore, and in this uncharted territory, maybe those drifting clouds are a map, after all, with their hydrogen and their oxygen, their quarks and their photons, those mysterious inner somethings that teach us what we already know, in our sparkling bones: that beyond morbid fear and importunate demand there is a way for this glorious concatenation of elements we call the Earth to align itself rightly and arrive home together as a single, sacred community.

BONES

Last week, I dreamt someone had hired a sky writer to send me messages. My name was writ large across the sky, followed by a private communication made available for public scrutiny. The next morning, I found bones on the path to the creek, three fist-sized vertebrae from some hapless deer that fit snugly together, like an intricate Chinese puzzle. As instructed by my dream, I inspected the individual discovery for its collective meaning, and here is what I found.

Each of our four seasons is three months long. Three is a potent number. Earth is the third planet from the sun. Plato thought the world was built from that three-sided shape, the triangle, and he wasn't far wrong, because the atomic foundation of the universe is, in fact, triune: protons, neutrons, electrons. Babylonians had three primary gods representing Heaven, Earth and the Abyss. Christians have the Blessed Trinity. Not to mention, three billy goats gruff, three witches in *Macbeth*, and the standard three wishes every genie grants to its liberator.

From three I moved on to other patterns. I saw five ospreys orbiting each other like a feathered galaxy. Puckered sand in the shallow breakwater looked like the crimped mountains and valleys of Appalachia, not surprising, since currents of wind and water and time created both. I noticed how shrinkage patterns make identical crazing on ceramics, dried-out paint or parched earth. How certain crystalline formations echo the mind-teasing structure of a labyrinth.

Curious, I went into research mode. In the Chinese language, there is a word, *li*. The character for *li* represents the markings in jade, the grain in wood, the fiber in muscle. *Li* means the dynamic forms at work in Nature, great families of structure that repeat in many manifestations. Aggregations, branches, fractures, ripples will cause similar patterns in bark, soap, marble, galaxies, on an animal's skin or within the secret architecture of cells.

Li is also a spiritual concept. When you're centered, when you're in accord with the Tao, you move through life with the same ease as dancing waves, which are like wafting clouds, which are like flickering flames. Your soul mirrors Nature's dynamic harmonies, the forces at work in trees, rivers, stars and the secret architecture of the human heart.

Yesterday, I fell asleep on the beach. The wind scripted its fluent alphabet in the leaves, on my skin, across the water's ruffled surface. Consciousness flickered, images wafted, as spontaneous and unpredictable as which combinations of hydrogen and oxygen will froth up into what dancing wave.

Now, the autumnal equinox. One season becoming another. The bones of the year interlocking with fish bones, dinosaur bones, the scattered bones of planetary nebulae. Some great organism rising from the muck of the universe. Animal, mineral and vegetable. Thinking our thoughts, dreaming our dreams, waking from our sleep to dance, to waft, to flicker through our private and public memories, scribbling messages from us to the future.

If I could read those letters, I would share them with you.

A Slow and Gentle Easing

What if we don't call it death? What if we call it a slow and gentle easing into what follows, and take, for teacher, this season of autumn? This began for me long before it began, way back in August, with one anomalous yellow leaf falling at my sandal-clad feet. Then, days later, another. Then, days later, a quick trip across the bridge, with a swath of treetops spread out below me, green whispering rumors of buried gold.

In that instant I became autumn's hunter, on the alert for signs of my still-elusive prey. Subtle changes in the slant of light. Night's small, inexorable inroads into day. A gradual crisping of the air, mind and body grateful for their release from summer's hot, wet embrace. The equinox came. The flat open palms of some leaves closed up into little silver fists, as if to grab and keep whatever had been theirs for whatever little while. Other leaves surrendered to color, to splotches of topaz, saffron, scarlet. Stains of eggplant purple, claret red, doeskin brown. The river turned blue. Pumpkins appeared in the fields, and corn stubble. Marigolds sprouted along walkways where brittle leaves scraped in every gust of wind.

Hunter no longer, that which I sought now avidly seeks me. Around any corner I can jump onto some dizzying carousel of color. Goodbye to the staid and stalwart greens of summer. Hello to paisleys, plaids, checks, stripes. Stippled, smeared, sprayed and splashed all across the countryside. If I grabbed some tree and asked it to explain, it would say, "Making food from sunlight is harder than you think, I'm just all tuckered out. My leaves are damaged anyhow, all those insects and diseases. I've sent out some hormones, they're making a wall between my leaves and my twigs. Without water, the green chlorophyll will disintegrate and, presto-change-o, pigments invisible all summer will magically appear: orange carotenes, yellow xanthophylls, red phycoerythrins. I'll need to store up every last bit of sugar, so I'll manufacture some anthocyanin. That will turn the glucose remnants purple, and when there's nothing left but waste products, the tannin will turn brown, the wind will carry the last of the leaves away and then, finally, I can rest."

Okay, teach, I've got it, straight from the horse's mouth. The world is falling asleep. Slipping from wakefulness into dreams. Losing its grip on the workaday business of productivity, turning to the necessary task of renewal. I wish I had time for that, but I've got people coming over for the holidays. Then I have to get famous so I can get rich, I don't want to die alone. I wouldn't be alone except for all these worn out behaviors, but they've been mine for so long, it's hard to believe things could be different. Trees have new leaves inside them somewhere. After all this dying, a season of fresh growth is bound to follow, but me, I can't afford the risk, and what would I dream about anyhow?

Raindrops in the River

It rained, briefly, then stopped, then started again. I thought, No need to dash for cover, this isn't going to last long. And stayed put. On the beach. Listening to raindrops behind me: tat, tat, tat on the stiff marsh grass, like tiny claws. Feeling raindrops on my face: tat, tat, tat on soft, warm flesh, insistent, a drum roll. Watching raindrops on river's surface, her face pocked and cratered. Tat: one drop plunges to its death. Tat: melts into concentric circles. Tat: lives again as flowing water. Tat, tat, tat.

By the time I got back to where my car waited – up the hill I clambered, into the woods I plunged, along the leaf-caked path I ambled – by this time I am softened. Tat, tat, tat. Ready to vanish. Tat, tat, tat. Melt into something else.

Now the rain stops. Silence. "Hush," the trees whisper, "Mum's the word." I touch my lips, checking, yes, they're all buttoned up. Thoughts are another matter. I do my best to let them melt, tat, tat, tat, into the thought-river flowing in my pocked and cratered brain.

I glance down. There's a ditch along the side of the road, clotted with leaves, filled with water. Dead leaves in a ditch, I think, but no, my brain registers a mighty fretwork of yellow and red and orange trees towering loftily, no, plunging down into sky to where gray clouds drift by, billowing underfoot, no, drifting high above, no, heaped in roiling masses and submerged beneath the swaying treetops that are reflected in the fathomless depths of a shallow roadside ditch.

I trace and retrace my steps, lost in the confounding shift between illusion and reality. If I stare at the leaves, the reflection vanishes. How mundane. Clouds above if I crane my neck, yes, a bit of fringed treetop, okay, myriads of gray trunks bristling in the forest, if I glance off to the side, ho-hum.

But when I gaze at the reflection, a dizzying panorama reveals itself, whole and complete. A majesty of multihued trees soaring together into a vast and infinite sky. Not the tat, tat, tat of separate entities, but the flowing river, and which is really real, I ask myself, and then I laugh out loud. "My me is God," said Catherine of Genoa some 500 years ago, "Nor do I recognize any other me except my God."

I'm still laughing now, as I write, because the moment was so vivid, so profound, and now it's vanished, and I'm stuck here trying to explain it. Something about me: a shallow, leaf-clogged ditch. Something about God: vast, infinite, contained by, containing all. Something about seeing the one reflected in the other, and something from my college psych class. About figure-ground relationships. Is it a vase or two faces? Is it a rabbit or a duck? Is it me, or God? Is it God-in-me or me-in-God? The whole is different than the sum of its parts.

I guess I have a choice, what I want to attend to, moment by moment, day by day, the figure or the ground. Because one way, it's just, tat, tat, tat, drops of rain, dying. Another way, it's deep calling to deep, tat, tat, tat, in a mighty river, melting.

Fossils

Arriving, I am greeted by their arrival, as they, in turn, are greeted by the shore. Kiss, kiss, kiss, say the waves, falling onto outstretched arms of sand. Home at last and welcome, after such a journey.

I know how they feel. It was just a two mile hike to get here, and yet I passed through epochs, startling thrush in the color-drenched, autumnal forest, herons in the marsh, and now, gulls spiral up and away as I look across the Chesapeake Bay from this beach at Calvert Cliffs.

I am a pilgrim. Sent by I don't know whom, to find I don't know what, but already kind strangers have equipped me for the task. That first woman along the way. She was trudging back to the parking lot with two tired children. I was aiming for the beach, wondering what a shark's tooth looks like, how on earth one hunts for fossils, and fossils of what, by the way. Because dawn tugged me from sleep this morning. Whispered a word in my ear. I'd heard about this place and so – obedient, expectant, trusting – I came. At a fallen tree I met her, each of us scrambling over in our opposite directions. A smile, a greeting, a conversation on the path. She described shark teeth. Gave me her daughter's sieve so I could sift for them among the pebbles.

Then that young man. He and I, both first timers, both holding our shoes, both puzzling over where to leave them. He had prepared for his visit with research, and gave me a crash course in regional paleontology. I shared with him my *chutzpah*, boldly suggesting we put our shoes together under the closest tree. Barefoot, we parted. He has disappeared around the bend already while I stand here, mesmerized.

My new friend told me that some 20 million years ago, Southern Maryland was covered by a warm, shallow sea. These cliffs that tower some 60 feet above me are the sand, silt and clay that settled on that ancient ocean floor, burying and preserving an amazing variety of Miocene-era fauna. Marine animals, mostly – sharks, rays, whales, seals, crocodiles – but bone fragments from mastodons, wooly rhinos and even camels have been discovered. Shells and shark teeth predominate, because they're hard already, more easily fossilized, and because they're abundant. A single shark will shed some ten thousand teeth in its lifetime, and mollusks are the sparrow of the undersea world: over 400 species of clam, oyster, scallop and snail have been identified here.

What makes a fossil, anyway, I asked him, and he happily obliged with an explanation. Scientists call it 'permineralization.' Water infused with minerals passes through the decaying object, substituting calcite, iron or silica for the original chemicals. Over millions of years the artifact is completely replaced. What remains is a rock-like copy. And here comes Elizabeth, soft flesh stretched over hard bone, a fossil hominid in the making, one day to be discovered along with her borrowed tool. Or not. Most life disappears without a trace, too fragile to endure into such a memorial. Like those soldiers whose faces I see daily in the paper. Killed when a makeshift bomb exploded. Shot by snipers. Struck by shrapnel. Beheaded.

After a few tries at the water's edge, I abandon my sieve. Poking through 10,000 round pebbles to find one triangular shark's tooth is a task far exceeding my need to find such a prize, and I'm distracted by the lure of other treasures. Color, for one. Right at my feet, in countless shells and rocks. Gray like iron, like steel, like storm clouds. Black like tar, like smoke, like twilight. The browns of chocolate, toast, a fawn's dappled back, blended in with cameo pinks, pumpkin oranges. Three steps down the beach, and now the rocks are ebony smears and henna washes; the shells lucent copper, nacreous tea rose. Old already when the Palagornis flew, that extinct pelican with its 18 foot wingspan. Old already when the Megatooth shark swam, 50 feet long, weighing in at 50 tons.

I bend down and snatch from this 21st century beach an artifact washed up from 20 million years ago. By shape, by size, by mother-of-pearl glints: an oyster shell. Yet pitted with holes like stone, gnarled like arthritic bone, its colors faded to cotton white: this thing is on its way to becoming something else. As is this tree stump, turned on water's lathe into the very shape of sea spume. And these hulking rocks, printed all over with shell shapes, primordial mollusks stamped into earth's sealing wax. From the cliffs above me the boulders have tumbled, sediment from a Miocene ocean floor, changed into stone, returning to a Chesapeake beach to be chiseled by today's waves into tomorrow's sandy shore. Faithful Penelope. Day by day and year by year the bay's fingers of swash and backwash pluck at this palisade, unraveling an adamantine cloth woven by time.

Squatting at the base of the embankment, looking up, I count at least 10 distinct seams of shell deposits, each in its uniquely colored strata of clay or sandstone. The cliff face is a multi-layered cake, topped with a green woodsy frosting, but it's crumbling away even as I sit here, pelting me with bits of prehistoric earth. I've heard it said that one day, all secrets will be shouted from the housetops, and peering closely at a fallen chunk of sediment from the bottom of some primal sea, I think this must be true. I run my fingers along the blurred edges of shells, buried eons ago, now straining to escape their tomb. They thrust up, eagerly waiting for the one wave that will at last set them free.

As do we all, on our way to becoming something else.

Earth is 4.5 billion years old. Without making any far-fetched claim for algae, it seems pretty obvious that consciousness and matter have made some profuse and colorful blendings along the way. Single celled, multi-celled, with nervous systems simple or complex, organisms keep evolving. Reptiles, fish, birds, mammals, and now, beings through whom the universe can think about itself. Over millennia, minerals replace chemicals, hard bone turns to fossil rock. Spirit infuses matter, we share experience, pass it on, ask questions, draw conclusions, make decisions. Awareness grows. We change. If some dead soldier of today should turn up a million years hence clutching a weapon, might it be to the kind of fanfare with which we greeted the discovery of *Australopithecus afarensis*? Kiss, kiss, kiss for a forerunner of modern human?

I am for home now, pilgrimage complete for this one day at least. The wind that brings these waves to brush against my feet could have brushed against the face of some stranger on a far distant shore. A smile, a greeting, a conversation on the path, we don't know what awaits us. As I stoop to retrieve my shoes, an acorn falls from a high above branch, its sharp fresh green a surprise on the pale brown sand. I'm tempted to pocket it as a souvenir, but no, this seed bears within itself the gift of its own future. I guess I owe it one small chance.

Vigil

I waited. High up in the Smokies, where mist curls from the treetops like steam in a hot green cauldron. Where clouds stack up like mountains, and mountains roll away like clouds, rippling to the horizon in an undulating current of hill and vale, high and low, a pulse as regular as wingbeats, up and down, a vertical in-ing and out-ing, like the tide.

I waited. On the first night, dark blue cloud-tongs opened briefly, letting fall to earth a glowing ember of sun, but I saw no stars. On the second night, the clabbered clouds parted long enough to reveal a pearl white moon on a nacreous chip of pink sky-shell, but I saw no stars. On the third night, I rose at midnight, peering past black lace leaves onto an unfurling bolt of ebony velvet. From tree to tree I heard the antiphonal chant of crickets and frogs, but I saw no stars.

Six nights I waited. Flesh of my flesh, I thought, bone of my bones. Elemental ovens, where carbon, nitrogen and oxygen were synthesized, released, refashioned, relinquished, formed all over again then set free to make all the planets and every manner of thing inhabiting them. Billions of years up and down, infinity's wingbeats, billions of years in and out, a cosmic tide. How I longed to see them, my ancestors, my companions, my guides. Six nights I waited, and on the seventh day, it was time to come home, where artificial light has long since replaced starshine in the nighttime sky.

The word 'vigil' means 'awake, alert, watchful.' There are formal times set aside for such watchfulness – on the eve of special festivals or holy days. There are times when life makes spontaneous demands of alertness from us – at the bedside of a sick child, a dying friend. On the eve of Yom Kippur, the Jewish holy day celebrated in autumn, the congregation prays, "May all the people of Israel be forgiven, including the strangers who live in their midst, for all the people are at fault."

When I was in North Carolina, I kept my evening vigils, praying to see the stars. By day I drove on steep narrow roads through a thick cloth woven from sunlight and shade, embroidered with the sounds of birds and insects. I drove through the V-shaped folds, up and down, in and out, thinking of the Cherokee people who had lived in those mountains for 10,000 years, until, coveting what belonged to others by virtue of ancestral gift, the strangers living in their midst claimed the land as their own. Back into the thick cloth that is Southern Maryland, my pen stitches the names of the people who lived here for 10,000 years – Patuxents, Piscataways, Nanjemoys, Mattapanys, Wicomicoes, Portopacos, Mattawomans, Chapticos – until we took the land they lived on, and their inheritance became ours.

Now we celebrate Columbus Day. Guided by the stars, Columbus made his voyage of discovery and stumbled on this continent. The stars guide us still, for tomorrow's new world is today being synthesized in the elemental ovens of all the peoples' hearts. Flesh of my flesh, bone of my bone, we are learning to say to each other, to our Earth. Everyone at fault, everyone forgiven, everyone set free to begin a new voyage of discovery that will take us, not out, but in.

Shall we acknowledge that life on this planet is making a spontaneous demand of alertness from us? Shall we begin our vigil now? In the great cycles of day and night, there is a light appropriate to every work: the sun for growing up, the moon and stars for growing down. Tonight, as our eyes flutter closed and darkness covers the waters of our sleep. As all thinking and desiring melt away. Let us pray for something deeper than thought or desire: that Earth's own wanting will take hold of us, that the Earth's own dream for herself will take shape within us. So that tomorrow, as our eyes flutter open, we can say, "Let there be light."

Baking for the Holidays

"Lay me down like a stone, raise me up like bread." As prayers go, this one's a champ, don't you think? I picked it up from a character in Tolstoy's *War and Peace* some thirty years ago. Still murmur it at night before drifting off into sleep, that dark oven that bakes us new again each morning.

Yes, and it's October already. Time to prepare for winter's dark oven. Time to befriend the night. From my deck I see her stride towards me, earlier each evening: arms outstretched, palms held open in surrender and supplication. From my deck I listen to her song: the stars and the crickets, a soprano of vast distances, an alto of all that is near and dear, yes, it is good to get to know this woman, darkness, for isn't she our mother? It seems so, at dusk, when lengthening shadows hurry to the solace of her breast. Or at dawn, when all things reluctantly depart the refuge of her silhouette.

Out in space, the sky is always black, for there's no atmosphere, no dust or gas molecules to absorb or reflect light's waves. Out in space, it's always silent, for there's no medium through which sound's waves can travel. Out in space, it's almost always cold, the objects that could conduct or radiate heat so few, so far between. Out in space is where our Earth is planted, who could forget it, with cold dark silent winter coming on?

Yesterday I woke up earlier than the sun. From my deck I watched night's beloved, inmost mystery become tangible in the day's affairs. As an incoming tide of light submerged the stars like pebbles on a beach, all the known and familiar configurations emerged: bird calls and traffic and a laughing child, the comforting evidence of routine and rational thought. Yet when I went to the store, it was magic and unreason that overflowed the aisles in festoons of orange and black.

We call it Halloween, but for the ancient Celts it was *Samhain*, 'summer's end.' Their New Year began with winter on November 1st, so October 31st was their New Year's Eve, a moment outside of time when the natural order of the universe dissolved back into primordial chaos before righting itself again. The dead could walk the earth that night, their strange and otherworldly soprano blending with our close, familiar alto.

"Lay me down like a stone, raise me up like bread." As prayers go, this one's perfect for the season. First comes Halloween, that riotous, phantasmagoric celebration of everything we fear and can't understand. That should soften us up a bit. Next comes cozy Thanksgiving. No need to fret the constant plunge through cold dark silent space, because Thanksgiving's warm and loving hands will knead us.

Finally, winter's long sleep. May we go in as dough, spirit and flesh. Come out next spring, body and soul newly risen. And if anybody asks, please say you picked up that prayer from me.

Joe's Garden

At the party, Joe's table contribution was two grocery sacks stuffed with salad greens, cucumbers, carrots and radishes, which I ignored when filling my plate because I hate cold crunchy food. But everywhere I turned that night, there was Joe, talking about his produce with the enthusiasm of a first-time astronaut just back from a stroll on the moon. "I want to see your garden," I said, and that's how I, maven of the frozen entree, ended up at Joe's place last week.

I hear us now. Me, giggling. Joe's voice, exuberant. "Look at this," he exclaims, "Chinese Red Meat Radish." He whips out his pocket knife and slices into the white roundness. "It's magenta inside, have you ever seen anything so beautiful?" I murmur an appreciative "No," and Joe continues, "It tastes every bit as good as it looks, sweet, crisp, great for stir-fries, and over here." He points up the row, "German Heirloom Radish, more pungent." Tenderly brushing back the mounded dirt, he sighs, "See that green shoulder? And this." I hold my breath to the silent drum roll. "Black Spanish Radish." Triumphant, he holds aloft a verdant sheaf from which dangles an ebony globe. "Grated, sliced, raw, fabulous with lentil soup," he boasts. I make a sound I hope is sufficiently admiring of such versatility.

Over the next hour we will wend our way up and down the long rows, where every plant took seed first in Joe's heart and he knows them as a mother knows the children of her womb. With him I will rave over the collard leaves, which look like some flower's wild, green dream. I will wrinkle my brow, wondering, Will that tiny cabbage make it before first frost?

Joe's friend, Mike, is in the far field, plucking kale to make Southern Maryland stuffed ham for Thanksgiving. Joe will call out, "Make sure you get some broccoli, it's absolutely gorgeous!" He will stoop down, straighten, place a rock in my open palm. "Part of the beauty of gardening here," he says. "This land was settled long before we arrived." The rock is triangular, knapped to a sharp point, notched at the broad end. My forefinger curls into the groove, brain slowly registering what hand had instantly learned: a fine digging tool.

It smells like the dirt it came from, seed-like promise of something both urgent and unfathomable. Shaped like a heart? A womb? I imagine I am the ancestor who wielded it, readying my store of implements for spring, which will be long in the coming but the season of growth will arrive, and from planting to harvest I will know, even as I am known: a unique and irreplaceable beauty. Worthy of love and admiration.

And if this is what we all want, isn't this also what we could give birth to? The whole world to be our carefully tended, our bounteous, our infinitely diverse, oh-so versatile and generously shared garden?

Maybe I'll meet you at the party.

Snow Geese and Other Considerations

I am on Assateague Island. The Virginia side, near Chincoteague, not the Maryland side near Ocean City. Before me, the eastern sky and the Atlantic Ocean stretch to reach their private infinities as I watch the horizon, where their and my separate desires for eternity seem to converge.

Behind me, a flock of snow geese is feeding in the marsh. From time to time, for reasons known only to themselves, they rise up as one body, wheel above me then out over the ocean, honking and screeching, black-tipped wings flapping furiously, white bodies gleaming in the wan sunlight that oozes through black-tipped storm clouds. Then they return to the marsh to feed quietly for a while, until, suddenly, it's up and out and over once again.

Beside and all around me, sandpipers scurry into the surf, almost but not quite into the water, then back up onto dry sand again, as if they can't bear the thought of getting their spindly little legs wet. I watch them in this perpetual dance as they search for invertebrates – has anyone ever seen a sandpiper sit still? – and I'm reminded of something my college philosophy professor said once. A classmate must have asked him how to define infinity, because I remember him standing stock still at the front of the room for a minute, then stuffing his hands into his jacket pockets while intoning, with casual surety, "Infinity. Never an end, always a next."

Today's grays are like that. Never an end to their variations, always a next. These clouds. Silver merging to ash melting into granite. The sea. Mercury sliding into lead into molten steel. The surf. Ivory frothing into eggshell spewing into pearl. Gray becoming white becoming gray again. Never an end, always a next.

They say this island was sacred to the Native American Woodland tribes – the Assateagues, Choptanks, Nanticokes. They considered it to be a portal where souls entered or exited the earth plane. Maybe that explains the mysterious comings and goings of the snow geese, which are ceremoniously rising to greet an incoming – or to say farewell to a departing – soul. I wouldn't be at all surprised, I can almost feel it: infinity lying all around, up for grabs in any of the countless shells arriving and departing this shore.

Mariners used to call this place "The Graveyard." The unpredictable merging of two strong currents in the Atlantic – cold water pouring south from Labrador, the warm Gulf Stream thrusting north – caused endless shipwrecks, apparently, and we who are navigating through the year, having reached this month of November, might do well to take stock of our own yearnings: The cold currents of that we have yet to attain; the warmer eddies of that for which we can already be grateful. Never an end, always a next. Infinity lying all around, up for grabs.

Thanksgiving Reverie

On any map, St. Mary's County, Maryland is clearly a peninsula formed by three rivers and the Chesapeake Bay. But it's not the map that makes it ours, this land, this peninsula, this long, narrow trestle table heavy laden with such rich and bounteous fare. It's that we come to the table to sup together on what, together, we have been given.

The gift of water. Like silver or silk or tumbling jazz notes. In diamond dashes or foam-flecked tiers. In sheets of lead, on cloudy days, or pocked and roughened by some storm.

The gift of sky. How legion, those blues: azure, cerulean, cornflower, Wedgwood, robin's egg, sapphire. How changeable, those clouds: wisps, tatters, billows, or even, at sunset, carnelian paving stones.

The gift of earth, whether carefully cultivated (lawn, field, rose arbor) or wild and profuse (thick woods, ivy-clotted cliffs, leaping deer).

In college, our class read "Ode on a Grecian Urn" by John Keats. I clearly remember scoffing at those famous last two lines: "'Beauty is truth, truth beauty,' – that is all/Ye know on earth, and all ye need to know." How stupid, I thought. How can people say this guy's a great poet, I wondered, when he's foisting nonsense off on us like something we can rely on?

I was young, and angry. I wanted life to make sense – it didn't. I wanted certainty – none could be found. Keats' words disappointed me, epitomizing all the broken promises and frustrated hopes the world had so far proffered, so I marched off to find a more substantial truth.

Flash forward. This current November day. I'm walking somewhere, and I'm startled by the vivid purple tips of a seed-blown thistle flower. Or maybe I'm driving, and the shape of a drifting cloud catches me off-guard. Or I'm sitting in my back yard, and some bird pipes up with a burst of song, and for one instant I'm freed from my tiny self's illusory baggage of broken promises and frustrated hopes, catapulted to a place that's large and real and true. I need to name it, the place where I've been, so I smile and think, "O, that's beautiful."

Flash back. 1621. Plymouth, Massachusetts. A harvest festival. A handful of immigrants and native-born folk, come together to sup on what, together, they have been given. Never mind the table, heavy laden with bounteous fare; it's the place that really matters, because the beauty in which we dwell is the truth that dwells within us. It's the American Dream. It's the American challenge. It's the one thing that can take us beyond red or blue states of mind, beyond politicians' broken promises or the frustrated hopes of bogus social agendas.

Flash forward. Some future Thanksgiving Day. "O beautiful," they're singing, from sea to shining sea. The native-born and the immigrants, the black and the white, the yellow, the red, the brown folk. Poor and rich, young and old, all come together – like us, today – to give thanks for what, together, we have been given.

Thanksgiving Hallelujah

Our ancestors – and I'm talking millions of years now, not just a century or two – our ancestors sat around a fire at night and told stories. Imagine. The sputtering red, hissing orange, flickering yellow. Just like now.

November. Driving down some back country road. The trees slipping out of summer's green disguise to reveal themselves as what they truly are: fire. Flames of it sputtering in the woods, sparks of it hissing onto the pavement, leaping licks of it flickering along stout limbs and spindly branches. Just like then. Imagine.

The sputtering, hissing, flickering blaze cooks your food, warms your flesh, keeps wild creatures away and is the only light you can count on to find your way in the enveloping dark. You huddle close, with others huddled close, all of you listening as one to a voice that spins the firelight into words, knits the words into images, weaves the images into a tale that reveals who you are, how you came to be here, what you can hope to accomplish before you tiptoe from the circle into the howling night. Just like now.

No painter could ever do justice to the color flaring forth from these trees, because all these tints and tones, these hues and tinges, they're not being applied to some inert canvas by some distant third party then offered up for my enjoyment, no. This moment is an intimate waltz, a sexy tango, a strut-your-stuff cha-cha-cha between me and a living essence. It is light recreating itself in leaf molecules, in eyeball molecules, light becoming a part of the tree, then becoming a part of me, then becoming conscious of itself, then rejoicing because it knows itself to be glory and praise and hallelujah.

Listen. My voice spins the leaflight into words, images, a story. Listen. In the beginning, time and space and molecules came forth from fire, a sputtering, hissing, flickering blaze of possibility and potential.

Beneath this disguise of skin and bone, our living souls are still aflame. With desire: the longing, craving, needing, demanding, wanting. With hope: believing desire can be fulfilled. Listen. It's a very long story, so I'll skip to now, Thanksgiving Day 2008, and I'll tell you what I think. No, scratch that, I'll tell you how I feel.

If I had a galaxy-sized table. If I were to place in the center of my table a cornucopia the size of the planet Earth. I would fill my trumpet-shaped basket with smiles. The smiles I saw on the faces of men, women and children all around the world, rejoicing because an African American had been elected president of the United States. I would add the sweat of all the people who came to America in chains. And the tears of the first Americans, who were driven from their land so that others could call it home. And the hidden anguish of all the trees chopped down so that concrete expressways might flourish. Then I would mix in the determination of anyone who ever arrived on these shores, having left a place where possibility seemed extinguished.

And then I would give thanks. For this amazing moment when we can gather around the living flame of our longings, cravings, needings, demandings, wantings. To tell ourselves, once again, in words and images, the story of who we are and how we came to be here. Because the American Dream is not some paint to be applied to the inert canvas of other countries around the world, no. It's an invitation. To every person on Earth. Whatever tint or tone or hue or tinge your living light of hope may be, now is the time to do an intimate waltz or a sexy tango or a strut-your-stuff cha-cha-cha with it. Because each of us is a glory and a praise, with something important to do before we tiptoe from the circle, and together we are hallelujah, a sputtering, hissing, flickering blaze of possibility and potential. In this new beginning.

The Moon of My Belonging

Who can lay claim to the moon? Despite the footsteps imprinted in her dust and the flags hanging limp above her windless surface, the moon belongs to all humankind. So says the United Nations in a 1967 treaty which forbids individual nations from appropriating parts of the moonscape, but fails to exclude private ownership. A surprising number of people have tried to take advantage of this loophole, insisting on their right to buy, sell, swap or otherwise profit from an exchange of extraterrestrial real estate. You laugh? So did I. But then the sadness kicked in: human nature at its avaricious worst.

Quick! Make a list of book or song or movie titles with the word 'moon' in them. This chuck of lifeless rock carries our hearts and longings with her on her 28 day journey. She governs our plantings and our thievings, our emotions and our tides. Earth spins round and round. Earth's oceans spin round and round. Heaping up towards the moon, emptying out away from the moon. Increasing with her light, diminishing with her strength. High tide, low tide. Lunar push, lunar pull.

Through my lifetime I have known three moons. In New York City I could hardly find her among the street lights. Amidst the ebb and flow of traffic and ambition, what power could the moon possess?

In the high desert of northern New Mexico, the moon was sterling silver in an onyx sky. I gauged her size with words I'd formerly reserved for olives: gargantuan, colossal, mammoth. She gave me a house of baked clay. Plunked me down in a barren, cratered landscape uncannily like her own: the white sandstone of *Plaza Blanca*. Flecked with silver mica. Pocked with ancient rocks. Even at her first quarter, the very ground swelled with light. By the full, I, who had once dismissed the moon, learned my own insignificance.

Now I live in St. Mary's County, Maryland, which juts into the Chesapeake Bay across three rivers like a long narrow pier. The sky is a blue-black mussel shell; the moon, its mother-of-pearl glow. Rising over our rippled, wavering waters, she sees herself reflected in a thousand silver chips. Hears herself discussed in a thousand conversations between soft night breezes and sea grass, murmuring insects and creaking pines, dry leaves and prowling critters, waves and the foam-gilt shore.

This is her family. She is at home here. Her magnetic fingers twine throughout our countryside, pulling at our rivers, tugging at our creeks. At the syzygy, the new and the full, the moon's face turns directly on us and we receive the abundant spring tides. At the quadrature, when her face slants away, our neap tides are scanty. More reliable than any legal contract, these risings and fallings. A treasure continually replenishing itself. An inheritance beyond price.

Who can lay claim to the moon? In my lifetime I have known three. This last, over Southern Maryland, is the moon of my belonging. I give it to you.

The Barn

Hushed and expectant, they await their moment of usefulness. Tillers, plows, lawn mowers, arranged by size. Rolls of chicken wire and electric fencing, neatly tied. Nestling tidily inside each other: empty buckets. Arranged on a pegboard: hammers, mallets, screwdrivers, wrenches. A level. Work gloves. Even the rowboat seems to be anticipating something, off in its corner, under its tarp. Because after all the digging and planting, the hewing and pulling and pounding, after one too many an arduous day, the tired homesteaders will turn away, briefly, from their labors. Kick back. Relax. Enjoy their row up the Potomac despite the jeers of the other boaters to "Get a motor!" Powered by nothing save muscle and purpose, the homesteaders will explore the river where fish swim and birds fly and worms churn the sediment and all things arrive where they're going, fueled only by muscle and purpose.

And where have we arrived, with our motors? With our technological advances that can take us to the nether reaches of the solar system but still can't feed the population of this planet? 50,000 children will die of hunger today because you and I like to get where we're going fast and easy. That's 100,000 parents. 500,000 brothers and sisters, aunts, uncles, grandparents. They'll all be grieving tomorrow because you and I want our food grown, packaged and even prepared by others. I'm no expert on geopolitical, geosocial, geoeconomic issues, but I do know this is true: I take up more than my fair share of this world's goods. More warmth in winter, more coolness in summer, more comfort and convenience than I'm entitled to.

I'm not lazy. I labor diligently, just like you, but I've lost touch with something vital. The barn at the homestead is red. It's a tough, hard-working muscle with invisible arteries fanning out into all the fields, where grass feeds the sheep, and bugs in the grass feed the chickens, and sheep and chickens feed the homesteaders, who harvest tomatoes and squash and peppers and onions, then toss what remains on the compost heap to feed the soil on which the cycle depends.

What, then of the human heart, which is more than a tough, hard-working muscle? The dictionary says love arises from recognition of attractive qualities or instincts of natural relationship, and manifests as feelings of affection, attachment; as solicitude for the beloved's welfare, delight in the beloved's presence. I don't feel this for the food I buy at Giant, do you? After she puts her animals in their stalls for the night, my friend the homesteader calls out, laughingly, "You're good sheep!" Then she goes inside to spin their wool into warm sweaters. She frets over the turkeys she must butcher, and discusses her seedlings as any proud parent might boast about a child. When I'm with her, the rafters of my heart expand. All love's tools await their moment of usefulness as, with muscle and purpose, I set myself to the task of caring for this place of my belonging, this Earth, my only and every beloved.

In Praise of Surf

At Point Lookout, Maryland, earth turns into a sharp needle, stitching St. Mary's County into the Chesapeake Bay, and all along the beach, a snaky filament of white cotton surf tries to thread itself back into the needle's eye.

These waves. Wind beating ocean's drum skin thousands of miles away, wind switching on ocean's lamplight, thousands of miles away, wind gifting itself to ocean's embrace, thousands of miles away and precisely now, the energy that was wind, precisely and exactly here, the energy gifts itself onto the shore as waves of water, tumbling, surging. As waves of sound, crashing, dashing. As waves of light, throbbing, pulsing.

These waves. Even as they leave the bay for the beach, they depart the beach to return to the bay. The simultaneity of them. Not this coming then that going, but both together, coming and going, arrival and departure, the boundary between this and that, between then and now, blurring, in the swirling surf, blurring, in the watching woman, blurring, the waves and the woman, two tines of a tuning fork, struck, reverberating as one pure note. Call it eternity, or infinity, or forever.

Or call it love. On the way down to the beach, I passed a family out for a stroll. Mother, father, child. I asked the little girl, "Are you having a nice walk?" She replied, "I love my Daddy." I thought, Out of the mouths of babes! Love is the answer to every question, a perpetuity of give and take, the child offering to me what she received from her father, the tumbling, surging surf offering to earth what it received from air, giving back to water what it's taking from land. A triune transmutation of energy, endless in its duration, constant in its changeableness.

Yes, call it love, the surf, and hold fast to it through your days and nights. As you wake, with salty dream-fingers still clutching the pristine sand of your barely conscious mind. As you plod to the bathroom to brush your teeth, each footfall a transmutation of energy given to the floor from your body, from yesterday's meals, last month's crops and critters, last year's sunshine, all of that now offered back to earth precisely and exactly here, in each shuffling footstep that echoes – doesn't it? – the sibilant shuffling of waves on the shore.

In all your hours, hold fast to it. In the crashing, dashing cycles of grievance and forgiveness. In the throbbing, pulsing revolutions of mistake and rectification. In the comings and goings and arrivals and departures that crest, fold in on themselves, wash up onto your experience then wash back down into your memory, the boundary between this and that, blurring in the swirling surf, the boundary between then and now blurring, in the watching soul, the surf and the soul, two tines of a tuning fork, struck, reverberating as one pure note called eternity or infinity or forever or love, until all that surging, snaky filament threads itself back into the needle's eye.

WINTER

Prequel to 'Winter'

Almost, it could be a mist, a gray cloud clinging to the earth, but no. As the road curves closer, the fog resolves itself into a tangled profusion of bare tree branches. I marvel at the work of winter: to strip green flesh from canescent bones.

The work of winter. An odd thought. Intrigued, I decide my errands can wait while I make my R.S.V.P. to this unexpected invitation. Remembering a park nearby, I head there, noting that heaven itself seems naked today: blue-gray clouds on a gray-blue sky. Despite what I know – that each season possesses its own wisdom – I've always hated winter. Have always preferred to build of its hard-packed longings something like a tower from which I could spy, in the distance, the coming spring. Now winter proffers her hand in friendship. Shall I take it?

I park my car and leave it, like some discarded garment. I need to be naked. Exposed. Like the trees themselves. The path I choose – or is it chosen for me? – takes me deep into the woods. Or is this the framework of a house being built? So many questions, so few answers, and that, too, is the work of winter, I suspect. To strip away the green flesh of our assumptions, taking us down to the bare bones of perplexity. The framework of a life being built. Of many lives being fashioned from puzzle and inquiry. The house that is the life of the world.

This forest, now, is the gray realm of burnt things: ash, charcoal, cinder. Of hard, metallic things: iron, steel, granite, lead. And yet, something is revealed here that hitherto had been hidden. Just there, in the serpentine twist of a limb, the rope-like curve of a bough, the surprise of twigs flaring forth from the tip of that branch, like fingers on a groping hand. And there, in the bold lines or brazen angles of trunks straight or bent. I can see what living has done to each tree; I can see, in consequence, every storm, every wind, every drought. Good season, bad season. Accident, happy chance. I can see it all, and I am here to tell you this: it is all beautiful.

Deep calls to deep, the psalm says. In this skeletal wood, my own soul's bones expose themselves: the choices I've made, my mistakes, my regrets. Yet the marrow of me knows what the cold sap knows: the fundamental architecture of any life is beautiful. All our leanings and all our twistings, our fits and starts, our strides and missteps, it's all a hidden magnificence. Even when choice has been taken from us – through brutal storm or harsh accident – even then, something beautiful is being built. One life. Many lives. The house that is the life of the world.

I return to car and errands, startling a flock of small birds: black pepper swirling to spice a gray sky. I have clasped winter's hand in friendship, and glad I am for the chance.

THE FIELD

Wild birds and bent flowers in the weed-sotted, sapling-sown, straw-stubbled field. I drive by on crowded Route 235. Notice how it yawns in the midst of concrete and brick: flutter of peace, sigh of silence, one breath, one blink, it's gone.

Or not. It must exist somewhere inside me, because later in the day I can summon it. Flutter, sigh, breath, blink. Amidst thoughts hard as concrete, worries dense as brick, behold: an empty field. Space for wild birds and bent flowers in a crowded mind.

Now I look to make tryst with it, like any eager lover. Some mornings, a thick mist hovers tenderly just above the broken chaff. Some afternoons, shafts of sunlight turn tufts of grass into emeralds. At night, while I'm sleeping, my field remains awake. To embrace whatever errant moonbeams or wandering starshine might be lurking about. All these my field can hold – the mist, the light, the moon, the stars – because it's empty.

Consider the atom. Its nucleus – protons and neutrons – is 100,000 times smaller than the cloud of orbiting electrons that surrounds it. If the atom were a cathedral, its nucleus would be a speck of dust. The atom is mostly empty.

You and I, the moon and the stars, the birds, the flowers – we're all composed of atoms. We are all mostly empty space, no more solid than chicken wire, which derives its strength from structure, not from mass. Positively charged protons, attracting negatively charged electrons, that's what we're made of: electromagnetic currents circulating in a vacant field.

You think you're sitting on a chair? You're actually hovering 10 to the minus 8 centimeters over it, the electrons of your body repelling the electrons of the chair. Substance is an illusion. Invisible forces of attraction and repulsion arrange our world into visible patterns, and these forces need free and open space in which to operate. Emptiness is what holds everything together. Nothingness makes all somethings possible.

Now we've come to the season of merry and sparkle and flash. Of buy and give and do and go filling every nook and cranny of every day and every night. If December were an atom, it would collapse in on itself, puddle into nothingness because of too much something. Just the opposite of the season's religious symbols. Hanukkah: a purified temple newly open to receive worshipers. Christmas: an empty manger waiting for a newborn babe.

And what about us? My field is slated for development, soon to be filled with more of the same, the same, the same. No room at that inn anymore, no space for flutter or sigh, no echo to the silent, holy nothingness that makes possible all our somethings. Where will they play, the invisible forces that give rise to our visible patterns, to moonbeams and starshine and people who open empty arms to embrace each other? Unless we find a way – Find a way! – to keep some fields free for wild birds and bent flowers and you and me.

Catching the Light

Blue skies and brittle cold at Myrtle Point that day. Threading my way past twisted stalks of sea oats, with the stubble of marsh grass underfoot, and the small surf cascading along the beach in falling dominos of sound. Mesmerized by the sparkling strokes of sun's pen crosshatched on water's crumpled surface. Dazed by a shimmering ribbon of wet sand curled along the shoreline. Glimmering motes of seedstuff in the air. Glinting insect wings. Flashing filaments of spider-silk anchored to the bushes, floating in the breeze, invisible except in this one shining moment, when, just so, they catch the light.

Then I saw them, freshly minted by the ebbing tide. I picked up one, then another: glistening pebbles like frosted glass. I couldn't fathom why, but I had to have more, so I ran that day up and down the beach, rejecting anything solidly white, plucking up anything translucent, stuffing my coat pockets, hurrying home with my treasures, and it's only as I write that understanding dawns: carbonic acid in the water has leeched away their salts. Once opaque, these stones have offered their very substance to the river. Now they are transparent bearers of the light.

But the days grow darker. Light is ebbing, like the tide. One of my stones is oval, another, round. Earth's axis of rotation is 23.5° off vertical. As she treads her elliptical path around the sun, she points first her northern then her southern hemisphere toward it. Starting June 21st, the sun loses altitude in our noontime sky, and this inexorable progression of shortening days and lengthening nights climaxes on December 21st, the winter solstice, the 'sun still' day, when our star halts its southbound journey and turns north once more so that light, like the tide, can flow forth again.

Ignorant of Earth's tilt and the science of rotation, our ancestors were frightened this time of year. What if the sun keeps going? What if it never comes back? Rituals evolved to catch it, hold it, convince it to return, celebrate when it did. Today we know the sun will reverse its pendulum swing without our help, yet the Hanukkah Menorah, the Scandinavian Yule Log, the candles of the Christmas tree or Kwanzaa kinara: all our festivals during this season are efforts to push back the cold and dark with warmth and light. One of my personal rituals is an evening drive through the countryside to look at all the houses. So bold, those sparkles and shimmers. So brave, those glimmers and glints. So defiant, all that shining, when night presses close around and threatens to snuff it out.

This Christmas morning it will be fifty years since my father died, so I know something about the dimming. As do we all. Earth rotates daily at 1,000 miles an hour, revolves yearly at 67,000 miles an hour. Amidst all this spinning and tilting the losses keep coming, the griefs pile up, and what are we in an ocean of trouble but small stones scraping in an ineluctable tide? Rejoice, I say, and rejoice again, because in this briny swash and backwash our opaque substance wears away, making us, with every day that passes, more translucent.

Einstein himself said light is a mystery. It is pure energy interfacing with matter at its electrical and magnetic levels. The sun is our primary light source, but the arena of interaction which scientists call electromagnetic radiation occurs in and around all objects, including you and me. What if we go one step further than Einstein, and use another word for light: love. Isn't that pure energy? Doesn't love interface with matter at, shall we say, the highest level? So rejoice, I say, and rejoice again, because the tiniest act of kindness is a radiant force, invisible except in the one shining moment when, just so, we catch the light.

The Fulcrum

Depending on the moment in humanity's evolutionary history at which you choose to begin counting – cranium size? walking upright? use of tools? – our species is 2 to 3.7 million years old. The holidays on which most of us lavish our celebratory energies in December – Kwanzaa, Christmas, New Year's, Hanukkah – have been around for 43, for 1,673, for 2,162 and for 2,174 years, respectively. Not only are they extremely new, these feasts, they are also divisive, a continual reminder of heritages, the naming of which forces us to see ourselves as similar to some but different than most other human beings.

What about celebrating something we all share? Something that aligns us with mystery, and with those forces at work throughout the universe that have guided and energized humanity for all of its several million year history. What about that big fiery ball up in the sky? The one that gives us, you know, everything? Dawn, dusk, light, life, energy, you name it, the sun provides it, and on the 21st of December it does the most amazing, stupendous, monumentally meaningful thing on the planet: it stops its apparent southward journey, stands still in the sky, then turns north again so that our short, shorter, shortest days begin to reclaim their long, longer, longest status.

The writer John Fowles says, "There comes a time in each life like a point of fulcrum. At that time you must accept yourself. It is not anymore what you will become. It is what you are and always will be." December 21st is Nature's fulcrum, the pivot about which the lever of our days and nights revolves. I'm wondering if the 21st Century could be humanity's fulcrum, the moment in evolutionary history when we accept a fact that has grown short, shorter, shortest in our consciousness; that is, we will never become greater than the web of life through, with and in which we were fashioned. We are and always will be part of a single sacred community called Earth (long), called the Milky

Way (longer), called the Universe (longest), and this, it seems to me, is something we can all raise a glass to this season.

No need to shelve our Santas, our crèches, our dreidels, our Swahili dictionaries in order to reclaim our large, larger, largest status. Just look up into the sky on December 21st and say to the sun, "We are no longer diminishing, you and I, we have changed direction, and henceforth, we shall be increasing."

Blue Moon

It hung in the sky from sunset to sunrise, spanning the last day of 2009 and the first day of 2010. A quixotic event that, every two to three years, arrives now in one season, now in another, bestowing upon the month of its appearance a second full moon which, because it is outside all systems of lunar nomenclature, has no proper name and is called, simply, blue. On December 2, 2009 we had an oak, cold or long night moon, while on December 31, 2009, we had a blue moon which, as I've already pointed out, shone its uncommon light on the last hours of 2009 and the first hours of 2010, becoming, as it were, a bridge. A yoke. A hinge. Making, of the two distinct years, one indivisible unit.

Leaping from astronomy to quantum physics, I'd like to point out something else. Scientists can demonstrate in their labs that, while atoms are mostly empty, the emptiness is not really a void but, rather, a cloud of possibility out of which protons, neutrons and electrons appear and disappear. Matter isn't solid at all, it's a furling unfurling abyss from which substance manifests, and, according to Superstring Theory, the newest scientific model, all those particles as well as the gravity that binds them together form, not separate objects or distinct forces, but an indivisible strand of energy in constant communication with itself.

Leaping from quantum physics to a recent walk on the beach, I'd like to tell you about the dead heron I found. I felt compelled to spread out its wings, as if the bird were still flying. To stretch out its neck, as if it were heading westward. To place, in its beak, the dead fish lying next to it. Then I scrubbed my hands with sand, rinsed them in waves that flapped on the beach like wings, continued my stroll. Later, going back to my car, I heard a rifle's report in the woods. And realized: that heron had been shot from the sky in full flight, its dinner wriggling in its mouth.

Where did it come from, the impulse to re-enact the heron's last few minutes of life? I believe there was a silent tug on the strand of energy linking our bodies. You can believe what you want, but let me point out that the first year of the second decade of the only new millennium any of us will ever know has begun in exceptional fashion, linked by a rare and special light to the year preceding it, asking us to pay attention to that which is bridged, yoked, hinged together. It is not a concatenation of separate objects, this universe we inhabit, it is a continuum, an indivisible unit existing for a common purpose, unto a common promise. What is it they say? "United we stand, divided we fall." Patrick Henry and Mahatma Gandhi used it of their separate nations, perhaps this year we'll learn to use it of the continuum called Earth.

The Journey

When the sun sets. When the sun sets on my river. When the sun sets on my river, and the wings of gulls turn to white gold. And the leaves of trees turn to green gold. And the clouds turn into carnelian cobblestones that pave, east to west across trembling waters, a red gold road. Then, yes, I shall find me some shoes of gold vermillion. And a sturdy gilded staff. I shall set my feet upon this crimson highway, and before too long I shall meet the evening star.

When the sun rises. When the sun rises on my river. When the sun rises on my river, and an incoming tide of light submerges, one by one, the sky's small pebbles of light. And the leaves of trees emerge from silhouette. And the groaning onyx waters turn to flashing silver sighs. Then, yes, I shall know I have arrived, face to face with the morning star.

And yes, I think it matters, that my celestial assignation is not with a star at all but with a planet. Venus. Except for the moon, Venus is the brightest object in our sky, in closer orbit to the sun than Earth. First to appear in the gloaming, last to disappear at dawn. Alpha and omega. Venus, the planet named for love and beauty, who watches over our endings and beginnings.

In Roman times, the goddess appeared in many guises. Venus *Cloacina*, the Purifier, giver of peace. Venus *Genetrix*, the great Mother, who bestowed fertility on folk and field. Venus *Felix*, the Lucky; *Amica*, the Friend; *Libertina*, the Free; *Obsequens*, the Graceful; and, *Verticordia*, the Changer of Hearts. Venus. Our morning and evening star. Fashioned from the same nebula that formed the planet Earth, named for all our yearnings, watching over.

The sun has set on the river of time we called 'last year.' Rises now on the same river, called 'this year.' Pause. When you set out along this highway, where were you going? Are you sure you want to arrive there?

Take stock. Is there something you might wish to put down? Something else more suited to this journey you think you might wish to take up?

Get serious. It matters. All the fields and all the folk, all the planets and the stars, we're all made from the same stuff. Protons, neutrons, electrons. A trembling flow of atoms and molecules. Action and reaction. Electromagnetic currents that groan and sigh. One vast and mighty river, what happens to me happens to you happens to them and it forever.

Ask questions. The year is just beginning. You have 365 days, 8,760 hours, 525,600 minutes until it ends. Let's say today is the morning star, still lingering in the dawn of last year. Before she appears as evening star in the year's gloaming, what do you want to accomplish? Think. Don't answer off the top of your head. Don't answer for yourself alone. Look beyond family, neighborhood, country. Look beyond your own lifetime. One vast and mighty river, remember? What happens to me happens to you happens to them and it forever.

And don't be glib. Don't say "world peace" if you don't mean "world peace." If you're not ready to do something to make this a more peaceful world. And if you're not ready, admit it. Spend the year asking the Changer of Hearts to change yours. I'll do the same. What happens to me happens to you happens to them and it forever.

So when the sun sets on our river of minutes, hours, days, years. When the flow of atoms ceases for you and me. We shall leave behind our trembling and our sighs, and ready ourselves to set out upon a golden highway. To meet, face to face, that from which we were fashioned. Our alpha and our omega, the sum of all our yearnings. When the sun rises.

Notes of a Native Daughter[*]

Often, in the journal that is my heart, the only entry is a note about how the sun looked on the Chesapeake Bay that day. If it sparkled. If it spread across the surface like a sheet of silver silk. If it disappeared altogether into heavy leaden swells.

Other days are more eventful. Everything that's ever happened to me is there, in the journal that is my heart, even the things I would like to erase because they cause more hurt than I want to endure, or because they fill me with a sharp and bitter anger, or because they prove I am not nearly as good a person as I'd like to believe myself to be and hence, make me ashamed.

Last year I discovered something that warranted a long entry in my journal. The Chesapeake Bay has a hole in it. Some 35 million years ago, a giant meteorite crashed to Earth, gouging a deep crater in the ocean floor. Millions of tons of water, sediment and shattered rock spewed into the air for hundreds of miles along the east coast, and the resulting tsunami may have overtopped the Blue Ridge Mountains.

The hole has filled in over the eons, of course. Until 1983, no one even suspected its existence, because the crater – twice the size of Rhode Island and nearly as deep as the Grand Canyon – is buried 300 to 500 meters beneath the lower bay and its surrounding peninsulas. Acknowledged or not, the chasm makes its presence felt. Continual slumping of rubble within it affects the course of rivers. Groundwater is easily contaminated by subsurface salt. All four major earthquakes in the region were near or inside the trace of the crater rim.

Last year I made another long entry in the journal that is my heart. An African American was elected president of the United States. He was inaugurated yesterday, on January 20th, the day after we celebrated the

---

[*] Author's note. This was first published on January 21, 2009.

birthday of another African American whose dream has been inscribed in the journal that is the American heart.

I've been re-reading Martin Luther King's touchstone speech. I've also been re-reading James Baldwin's *Notes of a Native Son.* And I've been thinking about that hole underneath the Chesapeake Bay. After the meteor struck, the sea floor around the crater became a dead zone for some 3,000 years. King and Baldwin both describe the dead zone created by slavery: segregation, discrimination, oppression, injustice. The burden of shame shouldered by generation after generation of white Americans. The loneliness endured by generation after generation of black Americans, exiles in their own land. Everyone scrabbling for so long in the hard soil of mutual fear.

These things are penned in the journals of all our hearts, we cannot erase them, but we can turn the page now and start something new. I have on my desk an announcement from the *Calvert Gazette*, dated June 21, 1919. It says that "the colored voters of Calvert County" have taken stock of "the very valuable part they had taken in the war" and think themselves "entitled to some political recognition." Consequently, "they decided to endeavor to put a colored man on the ticket this fall." Political recognition of value and entitlement. An affirmation of equality. This inauguration is that, and more. It is, if you will, proof that life has been restored after a devastating impact event.

America will always be affected by her slave-owning past, just as she will always be shaped by the destruction of her indigenous culture. Forever we will be subject to slumpings of a particular kind of rubble, to unique subsurface tensions, to fault lines that invite inexorable seismic disturbances, these are our collective heritage. But something else is ours as well, yes? Something we've inherited as a people? It is the capacity to transform our weaknesses into strengths.

Martin Luther King prophesied that one day we would "hew out of the mountain of despair a stone of hope." Barack Obama insisted, "Yes, we can." Whatever shape the stone of hope takes, I am glad I'm one of 300 million Americans carving it.

Shadows

Don't read this. You'll end up like me, falling Alice-fashion through a rabbit hole into a topsy-turvy world. You'll never be the same again, if you manage to escape, which you may not manage at all.

Still here? Well, I warned you, so, okay, I was driving south on Route 235. All that flat, black, boring macadam. Those tedious, humdrum stores. I was minding my own business, you understand, neither wishing for this nor hoping for that, not expecting anything except more of what I already had when I saw a scroll-work, a filigree, a lacy marvel of delicate shapes splashed and spangled across the road. Shadows. Cast by the 3 o'clock sun beaming behind a strip of skinny, skimpy, barren trees growing forlornly along the curb.

That was the hole, and I fell hard. Flagpoles, traffic lights, cars, garbage cans... stripped of their detail and pared down to pure outline, they all possessed an exotic and intoxicating beauty. Mesmerized, I could hardly drive myself home, but even there I was no longer safe. My same-old, same-old venetian blinds turned a blank wall into a spectacular gridwork of slanting lines. An unremarkable collection of objects atop my coffee table changed a bland carpet into a fantasy garden.

What did I tell you? See? Now you're stuck, same as me, scoping out the nooks and crannies of your formerly ho-hum existence. Have you noticed? Depending on the angle of the light source, shadows faithfully mimic but hopelessly distort their originals. Thicker, thinner, longer, shorter, awry, askew, tilted. Objects get duplicated every which-a-way on any which-a-thing: a mailbox on a barn roof, a person climbing a chimney, why, just this morning a tree grew itself right through my window and onto my dining table, bringing a soft breeze with it on trembling leaves.

Shadows are the funhouse surprise hidden in life's serious underbelly, but they can have important consequences. Peter Pan risked everything to get his back, and its recovery inaugurated the journey to NeverNever Land. Where would we be without Tinker Bell and Captain Hook? Then there's that pesky groundhog, whose amblings make no sense at all, I mean, if the creature sees his shadow, the sun's out and spring should be closer, not further away, but the folks up in Punxsutawney, Pennsylvania have invented some flabberdiflap about a Candelemas Day legend, which you can check out for yourself, I don't give it much credence.

 A rain shadow is a dry area behind a mountain range. Sound vanishes into an acoustic shadow. The psychologist Carl Jung called the negative parts of ourselves we don't want to admit we have our shadow. He said real maturity only comes when we take responsibility for those ugly, unwelcome newsflashes from the soul's frontier. It's still winter, but when I walked through the woods last week all the multiflora vines sported bright new leaves. Is that a shadow? I don't know, Alice, it's just you and me together in this topsy-turvy world.

Everything Curves

Crimson, his dog was called. His name, I didn't catch, distracted as I was by the reverberating shapes: snaking shoreline; great rippled swags of water sweeping the beach, crimping the sand; undulating heaps of seaweed at the wrack line; crescent-shaped shells; the flight of gulls spiraling over the horizon's arc. It was cold. Hoods drawn tight against the wind, we stopped to chat, our distinct trajectories of interest (his, collecting driftwood; mine, notes for a poem) bending into each other, briefly, then arcing away, although I can still see the worm-eaten shard of log he held in his hand: circular holes bored by soft, round bodies on their serpentine journey through the wood.

Everything curves, it seems. The rounded breast of the robin, the oak tree's bushy green orb, even the space-time fabric, with its warp threads of length, height, depth and its weft threads of duration. Gravity itself is not a force of attraction but a curvature, the shape an interaction takes when a heavier object (our sun, for instance, or a bowling ball on your bedspread) creates a circular depression in space around which a lighter object (Earth, for instance, or a marble on your bed) travels, despite whatever trajectory it might have assumed prior to this encounter. How this affects the stream of minutes and hours I don't entirely understand, but I do know that, when I'm with my lover, time seems to slow down, to stop entirely, to speed up, then cease, utterly, to matter, for why trouble oneself over a measuring tool so erratic, so unreliable? Better to rejoice in the wild and gleeful spin, the unexpected shape one life takes when circling around another.

In the year 270, the Roman Emperor Claudius II decided that unattached males made better soldiers than those with families, so he outlawed marriage for young men. St. Valentine defied the emperor by performing such weddings in secret, and when Claudius found out, he threw the priest in prison where, according to legend, he fell in love with his jailor's daughter. The night before his execution, he wrote the girl a letter, which he signed, "From your Valentine." Both courageous and romantic, Valentine became one of the church's most revered saints, and Pope Gelasius I declared February 14th his feast day in the year 498, probably in an attempt to Christianize the pagan fertility feast, Lupercalia, the celebration of which included a large urn from which Roman bachelors drew the names of the young women with whom they would pair for the upcoming year.

Everything curves, it seems. Some priest spirals around the need of young couples to be married. Some jailor's daughter spins around him. The story grows heavier over the years, bending the space-time fabric, creating an ever-larger vortex into which more couples slip, slide, spin. Minutes and hours speed up, slow down, cease, utterly, to matter. Life trajectories change shape. The serpentine journey is rearranged. Hearts twine into each other, as on a crimson card signed, "From your Valentine."

Clouds

The language they use is not my language, nor is my horizon theirs. That much I know. And I know, too, that at any given moment, 10 thousand stories with 60 thousand possible endings float in my head, clouds on the wind of thought but if I. Just. Look. Up. I can be part of a shape shifting epic far beyond my paltry efforts to imagine or control.

What gets me about clouds is how every one is an absolutely unique and unrepeatable variation on an absolutely constant theme. As water evaporates from Earth's surface, the molecules latch onto dust particles floating in the air. Warm air holds more water vapor than cool air, so when those two meet – over, say, a mountain or an ocean – the excess vapor condenses into minute droplets. Or, if it's very cold – above 20,000 feet – into ice crystals. Clouds are visible accumulations of these invisible condensations, floating in our lower atmosphere, drifting with the wind. From space, clouds look like a tattered cloak hugging the blue shoulders of our planet. From Earth, clouds look. Anyway. They. Can.

Smears, globs, puffs, clumps, up, down, in-between. High thin veil, low thick blanket. A shred far away, a wisp close by. Floating apart, joining together. Sometimes tranquil, sometimes furious. So many outside factors can influence a cloud. Wind, light, temperature. So much is going on inside a cloud. Tiny droplets get warmer, bigger, maybe heavy enough to overcome an updraft, fall as rain, maybe not. The droplets combine, leave larger spaces between. Less light reflects, more absorbs, hence, those sunbright tops and shadowdark bottoms, that amazing range of seething whites and eddying grays, roiled by dawn or sunset to red, orange, pink, purple. A swirling, surging, pulsing aliveness.

Yes, that's it. Clouds are alive, the same as you and I. I know myself as I was up until this moment, but I don't know myself as I could be tomorrow. I'm all possibility, perpetually changing within, continually responding to changes without. Forces, factors, circumstances, people. A mutable 'me' in a shifting 'we.' Floating apart, joining together. An absolutely unique and unrepeatable variation on an absolutely constant theme.

I think we'd be lonely without them, don't you? Especially in winter, clouds are ephemeral companions, assuaging the emptiness of a vast and relentless sky. They add texture and depth and beauty to an otherwise flat and boring plane. Some people like to categorize them. *Cumulus* for 'heap,' *stratus* for 'layer,' a prefix of 'alto' or 'cirr' to designate height. Some people like to name them, populating the void above with a comforting array of familiar shapes: rabbits or birds or ice cream cones. Me, I'd rather abandon my own agenda and just watch. An alphabet of white and gray. A grammar of motion and rest. An exotic language of limitless horizons spelling out heroic tales of unbounded potential I can always aspire to, hope for. Available to all of us, every day, without effort or cost, if we would only. Look. Up.

Cardinals

A flick, a flash, a fizz. Dash of, startle of, zing of red. The cardinal. Color of my beating heart, pumping blood. Color of the flame that brightens my dark, cooks my food, warms my cold. Red. For good luck in China, purity in India, courage in Europe, joy in Russia, mourning in South Africa, success among the Cherokee, death for the Celts. Red. Stimulates brain waves, quickens respiration, raises blood pressure. Symbolizes danger, energy, passion, power, anger, desire. Used in brothels, on fire trucks, stop signs and as a bouquet to signify undying love.

Small wonder, then, that this little crimson chit is a state bird seven times over. Illinois, Indiana, Kentucky, North Carolina, Ohio, Virginia and West Virginia have all claimed the cardinal as their own, and I must confess, I've been smitten, too. My lips just can't help it; they need to stretch from ear to ear as soon as my eyes register his allegro arrival on branch or feeder. I love the way he's sharp all over: pointy crest, razor-edged whistle; quick, keen snaps of tail and head. Never still, this bird, never dull. Always a spark of bright and cheer, especially in winter.

In the 1800's, cardinals were confined to the American southeast. Prized for their color and song, they were trapped and sold as cage birds to European markets, a lively trade that terminated with the Migratory Bird Treaty of 1918. As human settlement changed dense forests into bushes and parks, the bird's range expanded, and now, wherever the annual precipitation tops 16 inches, he zips around on a feathered wavelength of 750 nanometers.

Cardinals are helpful. They eat weed seeds and harmful insects, including the voracious seventeen-year locust. Both sexes cooperate equally in child-rearing, not unusual in the avian world, but what is unique to the species is the way males and females share song phrases, stitching together their separate patches to make one melodious quilt. Not a bad model. Cooperation leads to peace, peace leads to joy, who knows where joy might lead.

I looked it up in the dictionary. It means "a vivid emotion of pleasure arising from a sense of well-being." The root word is *joie*, jewel. A joyous spirit sparkles, a glad heart shines, a ruby-red bird flashes forth what's hidden in the secret heart of the world. Season by season. A stun of scarlet on snow. A surprise of crimson on budding branch, in dense foliage. A fat feathered berry at harvest time.

So I have a plan. The cardinal will be my decimal point for happiness, my bookmark for gladness. Every time I smile to see one I'll remember to rush right out and share a song with someone, or beat back some weeds, or vote for universal health care, or put an end to war, I don't know, all it has to do is make someone feel a little better, a little safer, then, flick, flash, fizz, there's a dash more joy in the world.

We Shall Be Changed

The gulls cartwheel in ever-widening spirals, their cries scraping the air like rusty hinges. "Fly away," I think, admonishing them. "The river's over there; you don't belong in the WalMart parking lot." But the gulls pay no attention to me, just as, in New Mexico, the ravens in parking lots failed to respond to my telepathic chiding. "Must you parade yourselves on this ugly asphalt," I told them, "with such beautiful mesas everywhere around?"

It's the pot calling the kettle black, I suppose. There was a small country store up on one of those mesas, close to where I lived, yet I drove 30 miles to stock my shelves from Walmart's more ample supplies. And today? By driving a few miles out of my way to shop on Solomon's Island, I could have crossed the bridge and treated myself to a glimmer of infinity sparkling up and down the Patuxent River. Yet here I am with the gulls at Walmart, practical and pragmatic.

The other night, I was warming up before an exercise class. I overheard a woman next to me say to someone else, "You know that new shopping center? They're going to open a Kohl's." There was reverence in her voice as she uttered the department store's name, and her joyful anticipation was echoed by another woman, who piped in, excitedly, "There's going to be an Olive Garden."

Their obvious and passionate longing shocked me, because just a few hours earlier I'd been at the beach. The chalky white arc of a quarter moon swam in a cold blue sky, its shape echoed by the curved breast of a swan floating on blue water, echoed again by crescent-shaped clam shells, bleached white and littering the iron-hard sand. At the wrack line, the perpetual ebb and unceasing flow of swash and backwash had etched themselves onto an old tree stump, sculpting solid wood into fluid, rippled slivers. Earth, sea and sky seemed to meet in that moment, their boundaries softened as they offered themselves each to each to be reshaped, refashioned, changed.

People need food, shelter and clothing. But once we have the basics, do we then need more food, bigger shelters, fancier clothes? What about the wonder needed by human intelligence, the beauty needed by human imagination, the intimacy with mystery needed by the human spirit? Contact with the natural world assuages our thirst for the divine. Can brand-name stores or restaurants make the same claim? When all the land is gone, will we be happy offering ourselves up to the transforming action of asphalt?

So these gulls and I, we're leaving this place. We're going back to the beach, where we belong. We shall stand at the wrack line, where earth and sea and sky meet, and we shall remember that spring – with its rebirth of wonder, beauty and mystery – is not so far away. We shall notice there's a glimmer of infinity sparkling up and down the river, and we shall surrender ourselves to it. We shall be changed.

Keeper of the Light

Closely manicured by swift salt winds, cedars huddle near the lighthouse at Piney Point, Maryland. I stand on the pier staring down at the Potomac, where swift salt currents rush in and out simultaneously. The schizophrenic tide creates tense ripples on the river's surface, treacherous eddies in its depths, and just now seems to be influencing a flock of swallows, which zig and zag crazily in staggered, frantic flight.

I have no clue what might have drawn me here today, just that I've been thinking about lighthouses for some time now, ever since I read a series of journal entries describing the 1633 Atlantic crossing of one of Maryland's founding fathers. Furious winds, fearsome pirates, boisterous seas, smashed rudders. A ship that drifts "like a dish in the water, at the mercy of the waves." Sure, and anyone who picks up a newspaper these days will find echoes of that harrowing account.

I think I would have enjoyed my job, had I been keeper of the light here. I imagine gadding about during the day, collecting oyster shells in colors to match my moods: white for happy, gray for sad, ochre-stained for pensive times, lavender-tinted when contentment rules. The crimson flag of the setting sun alerts me to hurry home, where I transfer all my treasures to some shelf, careful to leave there with them my vagrant feelings.

All night I keep vigil with beacon or foghorn, as the weather requires, but my duty goes beyond flipping some switch. I picture them in my mind, men and women in their fragile boats, storm-tossed, afraid for their lives, their cries woven into the fabric of swift salt winds. They need whatever light I can give them, shining forth from the nearby tower, or shining forth from that smaller observatory, my heart.

I remember reading something in the *Washington Post* a few months back, about how happiness can spread among people rather like a virus.

Studies show our emotional state depends as much on others' choices, actions and experiences as it does on our own, and the statistics are counter-intuitive. A joyful next-door neighbor, whom I may not know well, can increase my joy factor by 34%, while a spouse's happiness will only bolster mine by 8%. This inverse correlation between intimacy and impact leads to some interesting speculations. It suggests, for instance, that in troubled times like these, I have a responsibility to keep watch over my own vagrant emotions, especially fear. I must keep my heart's lens clear, as it were, so that whatever light I possess – faith, hope, love – will continue to radiate out invisibly but brightly, reaching those endangered by despair's boisterous seas. And what if, by some small kindness, I can make just one stranger happy? Then the domino effect kicks in, and that person's entire network will get a jolt of joy.

Today's paper may bring news of schizophrenic tides, tense ripples, treacherous eddies, but I am the keeper of the light, and I have a job to do.

A Different Kind of Wonderful

Low tide when I was there this morning. The virgin sand smooth and gleaming, like a waxed wood floor. A heron, way down the beach. Long legs planted in the shallow surf. Long neck curling into her breast, making a tight "S," uncurling, making a tilted "C." An "S" and a "C," the first two letters of her call. "Scrank, scrank," she cries, harsh and throaty, when she takes flight.

So I'm doing my usual thing, collecting any object that grabs my attention for reasons that, crystal clear in the moment of reaching, become confused in the moment of possession. "Why *this*," I ask myself, staring at the umpteenth mussel shell I've plucked up in the last half hour. They're all identical: a luminescent splash of violet and indigo on the inside. Drab black or brown on the outside, mottled with white. Some are as long as my finger, others smaller than the nail on my pinky. I keep at it, my self-appointed task, eagerly snatching up every shell I find, then wondering what the urgency is all about.

So I'm doing that, my usual thing, when I see these three gashes in the sand. Like a trident, with the middle prong taller and deeper than those flanking it. One set, then another beside that, then two others ahead of those, and I realize, these gouges were made by a heron's sharp talons. I follow in her steps, placing each of my feet just so, next to hers, but then the tracks abruptly cease. "Scrank, scrank," she must have cried just there, harsh and throaty, and I pluck up the solitary, bluegray feather she left for me, as if pitying my inability to trail her into the luminescent air.

Now I'm back home, doing my usual thing, emptying pockets and bags. While putting all the mussel shells together in a bowl, I see that what I'd thought were white splotches are actually a mother-of-pearl lining peeking through. And that every bi-valve shell curves left or right. I sort them by size, reuniting the companion pairs, which fit just so, side by side, like wings, and I place the bowl just so, next to the seed pods I found last week, also companion pairs, a top and a bottom, but these aren't wings, they're little boats. Some curve starboard, some curve to port. Their deep, narrow hulls taper to a sharp tip at the bow and flatten out at the stern.

So I did my usual thing. Obeyed my heart, not my head. By letting the blind promptings of one moment's reaching carry me beyond confusion, I've arrived at a moment of pure and emergent wonder. And now I have a choice to make, what do you think? Should I hop in my boat and sail away? Or should I slip into my wings and, scrank, scrank, disappear, leaving you with a choice to make, too. Stay where you are? Or follow me into the luminescent air?

Rock Chorus

Today they are submerged by the tide, their voices muffled. Two swans swim above them, foraging. Listening? A solitary heron stands in the shallow breakwater, the blue-gray smudge of his folded wings echoed by the blue-gray storm clouds unfurling overhead. He does not fool me, this heron, with his fisherman's vigilant pretense, I know he has come here to eavesdrop, same as I.

I heard them last month for the first time. A winter storm's swirling skirts had chased the Chesapeake's waters out to sea. The rocks lay glistening in the sloping sand as if standing on risers. I knew they were singing the same way a hummingbird knows a flower holds nectar: by its own body's instinctive hovering.

I hovered. My beak opened to imbibe. All colors, shapes, textures, sizes. Each its own impenetrable and inviolate self, yet each a fragment of some lost whole, a cipher for the eons. Some may have traveled here frozen in the ice of an ancient glacier. Others could have been spewed from a volcano now extinct and crumbled to dust. Still others might once have been clods of dirt in Jurassic gardens where primeval flowers bloomed. Call them rocks, or call them musical notes: earth, air, water, fire. Composed by pressure, arranged by accident, and by time.

The sun was bright that day. I picked up one large stone and held it aloft. Shades of ox-blood, ocher, umber, shot through with black flecks, gray striations. The wet surface sparkled in the light, and a phrase from that biblical collection of love poems, the *Song of Songs*, shot through my head. "Set me like a seal on your heart," I heard the rock sing, "Like a shield on your arm. For love is stronger than death, vast flames cannot quench it nor rivers sweep it away." I put the stone back down among its fellow choristers, and smiled, and walked away.

In today's leaden light, the metallic waters of the Bay swell sullenly. The economy, along with other critical components of life on this planet, seems to be collapsing, and we can only hope our leaders are capable of steering us through this crisis. Crisis. From the Ancient Greek, *krino*, meaning, 'to choose, to judge, to decide.'

I am just a little clod of dirt. Some of my molecules were frozen in the ice of an ancient glacier. Others spewed from a volcano now extinct. Tonight I will go outside and look up at the stars, stacked in the night sky like rocks on a beach. I'll listen to the throbbing pulse of crickets, and I'll sing with them, for vast flames cannot quench love, nor can rivers sweep it away. And if by chance you should be eavesdropping on us, by all means, feel free to join the lithic chorus, because whatever decisions we make, we are making together, fragments of a lost whole, ciphers for the eons.

Still Night, Twin Moons

Sun and wind have disappeared this night, and it is still. I recognize nothing and yet I know everything, especially this wintry moon. This silver disk that leaves me almost aghast at such perfect roundness, almost appalled at such perfect brilliance, almost confused because tonight there are two moons. One above, one below. One in the cloudless sky, one in the motionless water. In fact, as I look around I see that everything is doubled this night. The uneven silhouette of the treeline, a little white shed on the opposite shore, a boat moored at my neighbor's dock, all are twinned in the river's glassy surface.

A palindrome is a sequence of units that reads the same forward or back. Words like "radar" and "noon." Phrases such as "Damn mad!" Numbers, for example, "16461" or "12/02/2021." Even DNA – those spiraled threads that teach all life how to grow – even the nucleotides of our genetic coding can mirror each other. A recent genome sequencing project discovered that a palindromic structure allows the Y chromosome to repair itself by bending over at the middle so that a healthy twin can replace its damaged counterpart.

Which brings me to the dark, still night that some call contemplative prayer. "For you alone my soul in silence waits." For a long time I used this line when I prayed, sometimes repeating it like a mantra, sometimes settling into the silence and just letting the phrase arise when it would. The sentence paraphrases Psalm 130, and I can't remember where I picked it up – a set of taped chants, perhaps? I've been praying it off and on for 20 years now, always as an expression of *my* silent waiting, always directed to a 'you' who is God. But just the other day it came to me, in a quiet, eureka moment: the 'you' is 'me' and the one waiting in silence for me is God. We are all palindromes. Our divine twin forever bends over us, repairing the damage to our true nature, but in the mesmerizing sights and sounds of daytime, how can we arrive at such deep knowing? Contemplative prayer is the windless, moonlit evening that allows me to say, as Catherine of Genoa said 500 years ago, "My me is God, nor do I recognize any other me except my God."

Which brings me back to this moment, sitting here on this pier. The curling shore is silver-gilt, a lavish frame, and the river is fastened to earth, mirror to wall. Making a mirror is a painstaking process involving so many grains of Silver Nitrate and Rochelle Salts, so many pints of distilled water and ammonia, much stirring and dissolving, straining and filtering. The glass must be warm, and absolutely clean, for the least speck of dust or grease will show in the backing and mar the reflection on the finished surface. Isn't that what life is? A painstaking process involving so many grains of struggle, so many pints of hurt, a stirring of joy, filtering of mistakes, the warmth of love and we become God-mirrors. "Now we see as in a reflection," says Paul of Tarsus. "Then we shall know clearly, even as we are known." But do we have to wait until some distant future? Can't we be who we really are today?

Like many another in this newest and most fragile of centuries, I am plagued by anxiety. There's a line in scripture, in Peter's first letter: "Your opponent the devil is prowling like a roaring lion, looking for someone to devour." My anxiety seemed just such a ravenous beast, I struggled with it constantly, until I borrowed a peacemaker's tip from the Buddhist teacher Thich Nhat Hahn: treat the offending feeling like a suffering child, not an enemy. Envelop it with compassion, not hate. Then memory turned up a very different passage, from Isaiah: "The wolf will lie down with the lamb, the calf with the lion will feed. There shall be no harm or hurt on all my holy mountain, for the earth is filled with the knowledge of God as water swells the sea." Yet we seem to resist this knowing, clinging to our conflicts, inner and outer, afraid to recognize ourselves, aghast, appalled, at our true brilliance.

A stone's throw from this dock, a solitary piling stands erect in the tranquil, moon-bright water. It's impossible to tell where post ends and reflection begins. Be still. Be still and know. Be still and know that I am God, says the psalm, says the wooden post, the white shed, the motionless trees. If ever I wanted a book that would tell me what peace really means, that book is here: peace means not knowing where God ends and we begin.

Deciphering the Season

Paleography. From the Greek. *Paleo*s, old, *graphos*, written. The work of the palaeographer is to decipher the writings of the past. Fascinated by the relationship between the human hand and the text it generated, medieval practitioners of this budding science studied the *ductos*: the movement of the pen while forming letters. They also learned abbreviations, punctuation, ligatures – all in an effort to understand a scribe's style, so they could assign to the writing a date and place of origin.

Today's practitioner – that would be me – is equally fascinated by the *ductos* that confronts her now: the hand of Nature forming letters on this beach. Date and place of origin is no mystery: early March. The Chesapeake Bay. But I think there is a message here. I think someone is trying to tell me something. I think I would be – what? Happier? Wiser? More complete? The stakes are high. I would be some kind of better off, if only I could decipher this text.

I kneel down in a slanting wind. Every jot and tittle is important. In the pale lamplight of an ice-clad sun, I examine scalloped frills of purple seaweed outlined in pellucid frost. Is this an abbreviation for some other, more familiar word? 'Patience,' perhaps? Or 'courage?' Snow dust fills my footprints from yesterday, which are scribbled amidst a flurry of gull tracks. Even I, a novice at this science, can grasp the gist: 'small part of a big whole,' that's my interpretation of these hieroglyphs.

And what about this crescent sliver of sand? The beach's arms curve open to embrace the waves, which hurry in to enfold the beach, and their joyful exclamations wash my soul as clean as the freshly scoured shore. This ligature – this one character made of two or more letters – I've seen the pattern before. Symbiosis. Give and take. Mutual benefit. I never knew it to be the very essence of this scribe's style.

Walking in, I noticed dead leaves clotting a ditch along the roadside, yet, in the skim of ice covering them I saw living trees reflected from above. How sap rises in spring, in the absence of leaves to generate flow through transpiration and cohesion – this is a mystery not even plant physiologists understand. Maybe the answer is in the seaweed jottings I deciphered just minutes ago: patience and courage.

Just beyond the horizon's razor-straight edge, earth slopes into a curve that would bring me back here once again, were I faithful to the journey. Circles and cycles. The *ductos* of the universe as text unfurls under the hand creating it. As with that ancient style of writing Latin called *boustrophedon*: right to left, left to right, like an ox plowing a field. Or like anyone who notices that another spring will soon be arriving, and we're that much closer to the end of plowing, but some kind of better off. More patient, perhaps, or more courageous? More ready to embrace, with joyful exclamation, that which opens to enfold us?

A Message from the Author

If you enjoyed this book, please help me put it into the hands of like-minded readers. You could

- o Write a review at your favorite online retailer.

- o Tell you friends about it through email, Facebook or Twitter. (Or be counter-cultural – meet a friend for coffee and a nice chat.)

- o Mention the book to fellow readers on blogs, message boards, and online forums. (Evidently, recommendations from strangers carry more weight than that of friends.)

- o If you have a blog, please review this book.

ELIZABETH AYRES is the author of *Home After Exile, Mirror of Our Becoming, Writing the Wave* and *Swimming the River of Stone*, as well as the audiobook series *Creative Writing from A to Z* and the audiobooks in the *Invitation to Wonder 'Journey' Series*, which are based on this book. She lives in Maryland's Chesapeake Bay area, where she paces shell-strewn beaches to pluck words from the soft salt breeze.

Elizabeth holds a Master's degree in Creative Writing from Syracuse University, where she was a Cornelia Ward Fellow. She's been hailed by *New York* magazine, *New York Newsday* and the *Village Voice* for her groundbreaking teaching methods. A charismatic workshop leader for over 40 years, Ayres has taught at New York University and the College of New Rochelle; at the New York Open Center and Ghost Ranch Conference Center; through Poets-in-the-Schools and Poets & Writers; in libraries and other public forums. In 1990, she founded the Elizabeth Ayres Center for Creative Writing, which offers retreats, online workshops and private instruction to a global community of aspiring writers.

Elizabeth's website is www.CreativeWritingCenter.com. You can contact her there.

THE ELIZABETH AYRES CENTER FOR CREATIVE WRITING has provided inspired instruction and supportive community to aspiring writers at every level of growth for over 25 years. The Center is both training ground and launching pad, as many published writers who got started here can affirm. The Center offers a variety of online writing classes, private instruction and in-person writing retreats that will help you become the writer you dream you can be.

You belong here if

o   you sense something extraordinary within yourself and need to get it onto the page;
o   you're tired of conventional writing workshops, with their criticisms and ego trips;
o   you want a seasoned guide and affirming companions on your creative journey.

Let your creative spirit soar!

Individuals undergo personal metamorphosis as they write. Their work then helps others change. Because writers play such a critical role in our culture as it struggles to evolve, we have created a refuge where creativity takes pride of place and aspiring writers are encouraged to grow to their full potential. The Center welcomes all who wish to express themselves through the written word, no matter how little or how much experience they have.

Visit the Elizabeth Ayres Center for Creative Writing

www.CreativeWritingCenter.com

or call 1-800-510-1049

Also by Elizabeth Ayres

What does home mean to you?

Elizabeth Ayres begins life in an orphanage. Her adopted father dies when she's six. Her adopted mother says she's a worthless piece of garbage. Her stepfather haunts her bedroom at night. Elizabeth comes of age damaged, frequently suicidal and headed for disaster, yet, through all the darkness, a mysterious 'something more' always beckons. As a young girl, she builds altars in the woods to commune with a numinous Presence that is both More and All. As an adult, she scoffs at such childish nonsense and sets out to find more prosaic cures for the loneliness that dogs her every step. Marriage. A convent. A search for her birthmother. Still it lures her on, that tantalizing glimpse of wholeness and belonging she had savored as a child. Finally and miraculously given, in the most unlikely place of all.

"Spellbinding and beautifully written. *Home After Exile* is an archetypal story of redemption that could change the way we relate to ourselves, each other and the planet."
—Annie Dillard, *Pilgrim at Tinker Creek*

"This new book by Elizabeth Ayres is deeply moving and disturbing. It's the story of a human soul imbued with dreams, hopes, terrors, confusion, violence and deep intelligence. Ayres opens her soul to the world, revealing an insuperable human spirit that remains—despite years of abuse and abandonment—infinitely free and deeply in love with the God of life. This is a book to be read slowly and reflectively. Ayres is a poet, an artist of the human spirit, whose journey through death into life bears witness to the power of that divine Love which carries us on eagles' wings."
—Ilia Delio, OSF, *The Unbearable Wholeness of Being*

For more information or to order, visit www.CreativeWritingCenter.com/books/home-after-exile.

Also by Elizabeth Ayres

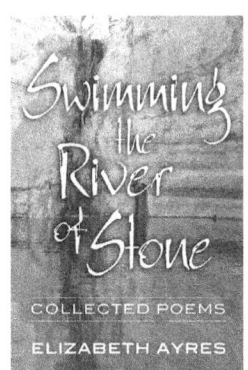

Paradox defines the human condition. We yearn for that which is good, beautiful, true. We're confronted by that which is bad, ugly, false. Still it beckons, our heart's desire, urging us to do the impossible, to resolve the paradox, to find the reality hidden beneath appearance: to swim our river of stone.

Written over a span of five decades, the poems in this collection represent one woman's struggle to find the 'something more' which holds out the promise of fulfillment and belonging. Some call it wholeness, some call it love, some call it God. Elizabeth Ayres has called it by all these names and more, over a lifetime. Anyone who feels drawn into relationship with a sacred mystery that reveals itself as the authentic self will find in her poetry a companionable guide in the quest for that "one, necessary thing." For as the spiritual teacher Richard Rohr says, "A mystery is not something that is unknowable. It's something that is infinitely knowable."

"The sheer grace and power of the language amazes me."
—Annie Dillard, *Pilgrim at Tinker Creek*

"Ayres is an artist of the human spirit."
—Ilia Delio, OSF, *The Unbearable Wholeness of Being*

"Elizabeth Ayres is Claude Monet with words."
—Paula Cohen, *Gramercy Park*

For more information or to order, visit www.CreativeWritingCenter.com/books/swimming-the-river-of-stone.

Also by Elizabeth Ayres

Where's *your* wave of creativity?

There's a vast ocean of inspiration within you, and you can tap into its power just by following the exercises in this book. Even if you're doubtful, intimidated, or blocked, the words soon will be surging out of your pen or keyboard, rushing onto your once-blank page like surf onto the shore.

Elizabeth's warmth and wit sparkle in every chapter. You get a personal writing coach who makes the creative process easy and fun while honoring its depth and mystery. The step-by-step instructions work for fiction, nonfiction, poetry, screenplays – anything your imagination can suggest, these exercises will bring it forth. And along the way you'll learn tools and techniques you can repeat again and again, whenever you want to write your wave.

Ready to take the plunge?

"Hands down, the best writing book on the market today."
—Annie Dillard, Pulitzer Prize-winning author
of *Pilgrim at Tinker Creek*

"Elizabeth Ayres has thought long and hard about the writing process, and is one of the most seasoned and exemplary practitioners in the field of teaching writing. This book is an invaluable distillation of her insights and experiences. I cannot imagine any beginning or struggling writer not coming away with some inspiration from it."
—Phillip Lopate, editor of *The Art of Writing*
and *Writing New York*

For more information or to order, visit www.CreativeWritingCenter.com/books/writing-the-wave.

Also by Elizabeth Ayres

Containing original material not published anywhere else, the audiobook series *Creative Writing from A to Z* shows you how to break through inner obstacles, unleash your imagination, and master the skills you need to become the writer you dream you can be. You'll learn

- o "Imaginative Layering," a breakthrough technique for generating limitless creative writing ideas;

- o "Extrospection," a powerful method for using your five senses to get "unstuck;"

- o "Structure," an intuitive, right-brained approach to organization that reveals the underlying shape of any fiction, nonfiction or poetry writing project.

You'll also find dozens of other exciting tools to help you overcome writer's block, take your craft to the next level, and jump start your imagination with the guidance of an exceptional teacher.

To listen to a sample or to order, visit www.CreativeWritingCenter.com/audiobooks/creative-writing-from-a-to-z.

Acknowledgements

Our English word 'gratitude' comes from the Latin word for 'gift.' The recognition that these reflections deserved to be published was a huge gift bestowed by Sandra Olivetti Martin, publisher and editor of *Bay Weekly*, the independent paper of Maryland's Annapolis capital region, in print and online (www.bayweekly.com). She was the first to print that which was first written. And by Susan Craton, community editor of the newspaper *The Enterprise*. She went out on a limb to make space for the 'Soundings' column. Rick Boyd, editor of that paper, also supported the experiment. And by Barbara Crafton, who has been sharing these essays with visitors to her online institute of everyday spirituality, the Geranium Farm (www.geraniumfarm.org) for several years. And by Sr. Catherine Grace, CHS, who carried the reflections on her *Grace-full Thoughts* blog (www.srcgchs.wordpress.com), then created and maintained the *Encounters with Wonder* blog (www.elizabethayres.wordpress.com) to give them a larger readership.

Friendship is a gift. Through all the ups and downs, ins and outs, steps back and steps forward involved in writing and publishing a book, these friends were present, offering encouragement and, often, hankies: Jane Sypher, Candy Cummings, Rhoda Neshama Waller, Janaki Patrik, Karen Karper Fredette, Jan Booth, Carolyn Egeli, Kellie Gofus, Jim Walsh, Mary Reynolds Thompson, Kristan Huthmacher, Candy Cummings, Helena Clare Pittman and Karen Karper Fredette.

Special thanks go to Sr. Laura Smith, CSJ, for her spiritual guidance; to Jan Booth, Paul Schulkind and Lynn Wyvill for editorial assistance; to my friend and prayer partner, Theresa Prymuszewski; to Bill Earle, the Project Manager at Accurance.com and to the entire production team at Accurance, for creative book design and efficient, courteous book production; to my cover designer, Karen Phillips of PhillipsCovers.com, for her imaginative cover designs and companionable working style; to Gabe Halberg of DadraDesign.com, for his stellar web design as well as his diligence, patience and sense of humor.

Companionship is a gift. My two cats, Sumi and Cricket, have been offering that for sixteen and thirteen years, respectively.

Love is the best gift of all, and Jeffrey Ault (1950 – 2010) made a significant contribution in that regard. *In Memorium*.

Reader Discussion Guide

The reflections in *Mirror of Our Becoming* group themselves into five distinct themes: the passage of the seasons; the cycle of yearly holidays; cosmic interrelatedness; the uniquely Chesapeake features of Elizabeth's homeland; an ineffable yet palpable experience of Divine Presence in Nature.

Here you'll be guided through five adventures you can enjoy by yourself or with family and friends, which is why Veriditas Books has included activities to share. Please note that each journey is available as an audiobook through www.CreativeWritingCenter.com.

A Journey through the Seasons

The recurring sights and sounds that punctuate our days form a great wheel: spring, summer, autumn, winter, spring, summer, round and round. *A Journey through the Seasons* carries you from flowering through fruitfulness, from harvest through snowy silence. Here is a series of questions that will help you discover fresh meaning and purpose for your own life's passages in Nature's reassuring rhythms.

> To listen to sample recordings of this audiobook, visit
> www.CreativeWritingCenter.com/audiobooks/
> invitation-to-wonder-journey-series

Song Flows Forth

- o The author says that "every dawn is another spring." What does she mean by that? When you wake up in the morning, does it feel like spring, or does it feel like some other season?

- Can you identify at least three of the birds that sing outside *your* window? Does knowing their names change your perspective on the place where you live?

- Young birds learn songs from their fathers, thereby creating "regional dialects." Do you have any distinct family traditions? Could you create new traditions to help you and your family feel closer to Nature?

Equinox

- Did you recognize the Christian symbolism in the description of the "downed tree"? Can you relate to that symbolism? If not, what are symbols of rebirth or resurrection for you?

- For the author, the return of the osprey each year signals the beginning of spring. What is your signal that spring has arrived? What about the other seasons, what heralds their arrival for you? Fill in the blanks: When I see/hear ___ I know ___ has arrived.

- Good Friday is an anchor in the author's life. What are some of the anchors in your life?

Reconciling with April

- April's answer to every question is, "Yes!" What state of mind – what attitude towards life – would such openness help you cultivate? How would that attitude of "yes" help us solve complex problems?

- Look around you right now. Find something beautiful in Nature, even if it's only a potted plant on a windowsill. How does opening yourself to that beauty shift your mental state? Could you spend five minutes each day cultivating a practice of beauty?

ACTIVITY TO SHARE: The practice of saying Grace before family meals seems to have disappeared. How about a substitute? Before dinner, ask your family members to name something beautiful they have seen this day.

o From what sorrow could April free you? Are there regrets from which other months might release you?

Praising Green

o How do you feel about green? Have you ever spent time in a desert landscape in which green was conspicuously absent? Did you miss it?

o As more and more green spaces are replaced with concrete, glass and neon, what do you think is happening to the human psyche?

o The science of the chlorophyll molecule here becomes a metaphor. Can you explain, in your own words, what lesson the chlorophyll molecule teaches?

The Zone

o Can people ever 'stand still' in life? If they try, what are some of the ramifications? What about a society? What happens if it tries to 'stand still?'

o Can you identify an area in your life where you're stuck and could use some "hazy crazy midsummer magic"? What would that magic look like? What kind of change do you long for? Is there some aspect of Nature that symbolizes that change to you?

o What about our civilization? Where is it stuck? In your opinion, what would get it moving in a positive direction again?

Berries Blossoms Bunting

- The author claims each object she gathers is a "crucial clue in a mystery I must solve." She also says these objects are "fragments of my scattered self." What does she mean? Is that true for you as well? Do you find some essential part of yourself in Nature? What is it?

    ACTIVITY TO SHARE: Make an empty bowl the centerpiece of your family's dining table. Have each person put in it something they've gathered from outdoors. Let your mealtime conversation include a discussion of the objects in the bowl, what they mean to each family member. Are there connections to be drawn between the objects and the collectors?

- It is necessary to plan ahead for our seasonal needs – warm clothes for winter, picnic gear for summer. How can you resist being unbalanced by the need to look ahead? What would help you stay in touch with the season that is unfolding around you right now?

- If you were to include in your next July Fourth celebration something to symbolize your family's "independence from an oppressive regime of commercialization," what would it be?

A Slow and Gentle Easing

- Are you a hunter? Someone who, like the author, is aware of miniscule seasonal changes? Can you look in your own back yard right now and spot one sign of the season-yet-to-be?

- Psychologically, is it spring, summer, autumn or winter in your life now? Does that put you in synch or at odds with Nature?

- What are your beliefs about an after-life? Is death a "slow and gentle easing into what follows" for you? What does autumn say to *you* about the passage from one life to another?

Joe's Garden

- o If you love to garden, take a few moments to describe how you feel when you're digging, planting, watering or weeding. How do you feel when you eat food or enjoy blossoms that you have grown yourself?

- o If you don't garden, can you think of some way you can incorporate into your life some of Joe's passion for and attachment to the earth?

- o What about your sense of connection to the place you inhabit? Can you name people who lived here 100 years ago? Can you name the indigenous population that resided here before you? How is your life richer or larger because of this knowledge?

Thanksgiving Hallelujah

- o There are two kinds of fire referred to in this reflection. What are they? Why are they important to the author? Are they important to you?

- o What are you grateful for at Thanksgiving? Do you incorporate gratitude to the natural world as a part of your celebration? If not, how would you begin to do that? If so, how might you expand on that custom?

- o The author makes reference to the American Dream in this reflection, comparing it to the way light and color interact in Nature. Can you find, in Nature, an image for what the American Dream means to you? How does that image express or influence your identity as a citizen of the United States and a member of the Earth community?

Making Friends with Winter

- o Do you, like the author, hate winter, or do you enjoy the season? Why?

- o In "the tangled profusion of bare tree branches," the author senses an invitation to a greater intimacy with the season at hand, and by accepting this invitation she discovers "a hidden magnificence" in her life. In your own words, what is the beauty that's revealed to her? Do you see that manifesting in your life? How?

- o Pick one aspect of winter: its cold, its silence, its lack of light. Can you "make friends" with that? Does it teach you something valuable about the times in your life when coldness, silence or darkness have arrived?

Cardinals

- o The color red symbolizes different things in different cultures. Pick a color that intrigues you. Where do you find it in the natural world? Search the internet to discover its symbolic meaning.

    ACTIVITY TO SHARE: Here's a "party popper" idea. Jot down color words on index cards. Pass them out. Each person (or team) must come up with ten ways that color appears in Nature. Audience assistance is encouraged!

- o Beyond the standard domestic animals, what critters do you especially love? Frogs? Dragonflies? Something else? What is it about the creature that charms you?

- o If humankind were to model its behavior on the being you selected above, what positive changes would result?

Deciphering the Seasons

o   Where in Nature do you find a symbol for patience? For courage?

o   In what season do you find the most aliveness?

o   The author refers to "circles and cycles" of the journey through life. How do you feel about aging? If you were more closely connected to the natural world, do you think your feelings about the aging process might change? How?

Celebrating the Journey

The festivals that recur each year are meant to enliven and inspire us, but sometimes they become chores. These meditations will take you from New Year's through July Fourth into Columbus Day; from Valentine's Day to Halloween; from Easter, Passover and the vernal equinox through Christmas, Hanukkah, Kwanzaa and the winter solstice. We hope *Celebrating the Journey* enriches your holiday celebrations as life-affirming occasions of wonder and joy.

> To listen to sample recordings of this audiobook, visit
> www.CreativeWritingCenter.com/audiobooks/
> invitation-to-wonder-journey-series

The Journey (New Year's Day)

- o Parties, staying up until midnight, watching the Times Square ball descend – these are some of our traditional New Year's Eve celebrations in the United States. If you were to begin a New Year's Eve tradition that somehow incorporates Nature, what would you do?

- o Most people end up feeling guilty for not keeping New Year's resolutions they make. Would it help if your resolution were connected to some aspect of Nature you experience each day, like dawn and sunset? Why?

- o How could you enlarge your celestial awareness? How could you incorporate into your everyday life planets like Venus and Mars, stars like Zeta Draconis, or galaxies like Andromeda? What difference might it make in your life, having such "friends" up above?

    > ACTIVITY TO SHARE: If you go online and search for "name a star," you'll find many ways to name a star after someone; some naming options are quite inexpensive. Or, instead of relying on those tried-and-true names of

constellations, invent your own names for the groupings of stars you see above your head! Rory Rabbit? Rocky Road?

Notes of a Native Daughter (Martin Luther King Day)

- o   In this reflection, the author makes a discovery about the landscape she inhabits. Ask around and see if you can make a discovery about the place where *you* live. Does this revelation influence your thinking in any way? Does it make any difference in your life?

- o   Do you agree that America will always be affected by her slave-owning past? By the destruction of her indigenous population? How have you experienced racial tensions in your life, described here as "the hard soil of mutual fear"?

- o   Do you agree that "the capacity to transform our weaknesses into strengths" is a hallmark of the American people? Why or why not?

Shadows (Groundhog Day)

- o   On February 2nd, in the northern hemisphere at least, winter is firmly entrenched and spring is far away. How do you feel during that time of the year?

- o   Try devoting one hour to noticing shadows – in your office, your home, your back yard. Does observing these "funhouse surprises" change your attitude in any way?

    ACTIVITY TO SHARE: Grab a friend, a spouse, or round up the kids. Declare the next early-morning or late-afternoon hour a "shadow hunting field trip." Make it a game, like Pinchbuggy! See who can spot the most, or find them first. The winner gets...?

- o   When the author sees new leaves sprouting from multiflora vines in January, she calls this a shadow. What does she mean by that? Do you agree? How do you feel about climate change?

Everything Curves (Valentine's Day)

- In this reflection, curves have caught the author's attention, and she notices them in the snaking shoreline, crescent-shaped shells, the rounded breast of the robin, even the space-time fabric. Decide on a geometric shape – circle, square, triangle, rectangle – then see how many instances of it you can find in the landscape you inhabit.

- During Lupercalia, the Roman fertility feast, unmarried Roman men would draw from an urn the names of women with whom they would pair for the upcoming year. Does this practice have parallels in today's Valentine's Day celebrations?

- Have you ever done something that seemed to make time stand still? What was it? How could you incorporate that activity into your next Valentine's Day festivities?

Passing By (Easter, Passover, the vernal equinox)

- In Southern Maryland, the crumbling tobacco barns mark the passing of a way of life. Are there any remnants of bygone lifestyles in your neighborhood? How do you feel when you come upon these remnants?

    ACTIVITY TO SHARE: Make a family outing to some "back in the day" landmark. Have your kids do a bit of research before you go – the trip will be educational and fun at the same time.

- Do you celebrate Easter or Passover? If so, how do you experience the relationship between the religious feast and the season? Is it truly a time of rebirth for you? Why or why not?

- If you don't celebrate the traditional religious holidays, what are your "here comes spring" traditions? Do you think your life might be made richer by doing something to formally acknowledge the vernal equinox? What could you do?

Maytime Musings (Mother's Day)

- o What outdoor activities help you feel uplifted, when you're down, or soothed, when you're anxious? In what sense are these "mothering" experiences?

- o If you don't get outdoors much, check your television listings for the next Nature show. Observe how you feel before, during and after the program. Any changes? In what sense is this a "mothering" experience?

- o In the United States, Mother's Day originated with social activist Julia Ward Howe. She wanted to call it "Mother's Day for Peace," and envisioned women devoting their energies to protesting war on that day. If you could find a way to acknowledge Mother Nature this day, would that be a step towards a more peaceful planet?

Remembering the Future (Memorial Day)

- o What does the author mean when she says, "We are all prisoners of war"? Do you agree that it is "our duty to escape"?

- o There are many kinds of wars – without and within. How might cultivating a relationship with Nature help you "escape" the war within? How might greater intimacy with the natural world help America "escape" wars with other countries?

- o As the 2010 Gulf oil spill demonstrated, there is a battle raging between humans and the non-human world. What activity could you include in your Memorial Day celebration that might symbolize the healing of this conflict?

Butterfly Q & A (Independence Day)

- o The author remembers imbibing honeysuckle nectar when she was a child. Did you ever do that? Recall one vivid memory you have from your own childhood that includes Nature.

- What hunger does "tippling honeysuckle" satisfy? How can this activity be "vastly superior" to the accomplishments you've been taught to believe are important? How might close encounters with Nature's wonders change your attitude about "what really matters"?

- The author here compares the American Dream to a "silky, too-tight cocoon." What aspects of American culture do you think should be discarded in order to make us a more mature society?

The Work We Do (Labor Day)

- Do you know what a 'bioregion' is? Do you know the name of the bioregion you currently inhabit? (Five minutes of internet research would be very fruitful in this regard.) What was going on in your neighborhood 12 million years ago?

  ACTIVITY TO SHARE: Organize a "Sense of Place" course. It's easy! Northwest Earth Institute (nwei.org) offers a 7-session course called "Discovering a Sense of Place." They provide nifty study guides for a nominal fee. Collect a group, find a host location (or round-robin in participants' homes) and learn to cherish the place where you live.

- The author here describes the way pound-net fisherman once worked in the Chesapeake Bay. What are the traditional forms of labor in *your* state? What could you do to incorporate such activities – or the memory of them – into your Labor Day celebration?

- Human beings are citizens of various countries, but all countries belong to a greater Earth community. What are your dreams for Earth? Could you include in your Labor Day festivities one small step towards making your dream a reality?

Vigil (Columbus Day)

- In this reflection, the author names the Native American tribes which inhabited her area of Maryland. Can you name the indigenous tribes that lived in *your* neighborhood 10,000 years ago? How might your life be enriched by such knowledge? Could you do something this Columbus Day to honor the people who lived here before you did?

- The author says the stars are "Flesh of my flesh, bone of my bones," a double allusion which refers both to the story of creation in the book of Genesis and to contemporary wedding ceremonies. What does she mean by making this connection?

- Are you aware of any demands that life on this planet might be making now? What are they? Could you include a response to such appeals as a part of your Columbus Day festivities?

Baking for the Holidays (Halloween)

- What is your reaction to autumn's earlier nightfall? How do you feel when Daylight Savings Time ends? What do you do at that time that marks the shift from a season of light to a season of greater darkness?

- After New Year's and the Super Bowl, Halloween is the third largest party occasion in the United States. Two-thirds of all adults will celebrate it, half spending more than $100, and consumers will send 28 million cards. Can you think of a way to make your celebration of Halloween more of an occasion for "befriending" the darkness and less of a commercial enterprise? Would you then feel more aligned with the season?

- The Celtic New Year feast called *Samhain* is a harvest holiday, and a night to remember those who have crossed over before us. How might you include in your Halloween festivities some acknowledgement of your honored dead?

Reverie (Thanksgiving Day)

- What does the author mean when she says, "The beauty in which we dwell is the truth that dwells within us"? Do you agree?

- How might an awareness of the beauty and diversity of the North American continent influence what we call the American Dream?

- How could you expand the parameters of your current Thanksgiving Day tradition to include appreciation for the gifts of earth, sea and sky? Could you, for instance, revamp your holiday centerpiece with feathers and shells, or fill a decorative jar with water from the stream or river closest to you?

Catching the Light (Christmas, Hanukkah, Kwanzaa, the winter solstice)

- The author says that in the "briny swash and backwash" of living, "our opaque substance wears away, making us, with every day that passes, more translucent." To what natural phenomenon is she comparing the passage of time? What image drawn from Nature speaks to *you* most profoundly of life's myriad changes?

- The generic phrase "winter holidays" is now used widely, but which feast do you actually celebrate? Does it have a religious or spiritual dimension for you?

- Kwanzaa, Christmas and Hanukkah have been around for 43, 1,673 and 2,174 years, respectively, but these feasts can remind us of an exclusive rather than an inclusive heritage. The solstice reminds us that we all share the sun's light. Celebrating it aligns us with mystery, with those forces at work throughout the universe that have guided and energized humanity for all of its several million year history. How might you incorporate an awareness of the winter solstice into your family's holiday tradition?

A Journey into the Cosmos

We are the universe becoming conscious of itself. Our journey began 13.7 billion years ago in a glorious throb of energy and light that recreates itself at every moment through the interdependence of life on earth in all its manifestations. We hope this guide to *A Journey into the Cosmos* will help you discover new images for reflection in science and new metaphors for understanding in Nature.

> To listen to sample recordings of this audiobook, visit
> www.CreativeWritingCenter.com/audiobooks/
> invitation-to-wonder-journey-series

Seedsong: An Elegy for Thomas Berry

- o The writer Wendell Berry says, "If you don't know where you are, you don't know who you are." Has any place – present or past – had an impact on your identity? Can you define that impact?

- o In this reflection, the author says, "It takes time to hear the voice of a place." How long have you been living in your current neighborhood? What aspects of Nature there – creatures, plants, land formations – speak to you most strongly?

    > ACTIVITY TO SHARE: Ask your friends, neighbors or family members to bring to the next gathering (meal, party, etc.) some small object representative of the place where they live – an acorn, a stone, a shell. Give everyone a chance to articulate why they chose that object, what about it is special or meaningful to them.

- o What are your beliefs about life after death? What aspects of Nature – e.g., sunrise, seeds, the progression of the seasons – could symbolize your beliefs? Do you find comfort in these symbols?

What the Light Calls Forth

- Explore your relationship with light by recalling the last string of rainy days. How did you feel when you first saw the sun again?

- Explore your relationship with the universe by considering: your body is 60% water; water is hydrogen combined with oxygen; the element hydrogen was formed in the Big Bang 13.7 billion years ago; 90% of all atoms in the universe are hydrogen. What does this mean to you?

- Joni Mitchell sings, "We are stardust, we are golden, and we've got to get ourselves back to the garden." What garden is she referring to? If all things on Earth – animals, minerals, vegetables – are arrangements of elements formed inside stars like our Sun, what small step might you take today to get yourself one step closer to "the garden"?

Ghost Ship

- We are the first generation in humanity's history to have an indisputable picture of the world we inhabit – the photo of Earth taken from the Moon, where it is clear there are no separations between "us" and "them." Find this image on the Internet (search for "photo of Earth"). To what "new and fuller life" does the picture invite you?

    ACTIVITY TO SHARE: Print out the photo of the Earth. Pass it around at your next family meal, or take it to your next party. Ask everyone to come up with one word that expresses his or her response to the image.

- Ask yourself, "What constrains me? What keeps me small? Unfree? Less than who I really want to be?" Can you let go anywhere?

- Now ask yourself, "Do I feel more or less free when I'm outdoors, somehow engaged with Nature's beauty?" Can you bestow upon yourself the gift of going outside *now*? Today? Tomorrow?

The Comfort of Green

- What does the author mean when she says, "From the green heart of the growing world a green pulse continues to throb"? In what sense is "green" an umbilical cord? In what sense is Earth a womb?

- How much "green" surrounds you right now? What physiological or psychological changes take place within you when you're exposed to green living things?

- Has the area where you live undergone development over the years? If income were not an issue, would you move to a more pastoral environment? What could you do tomorrow to bring more "green" into your life?

The Pier

- When you see something you knew as a child – a place, a person, an object – and compare "then" with "now," is the experience positive or negative for you?

- Think of a tree in your life, past or present. It could be the tree you fell out of when you were a kid. Or the tree outside your bedroom window right now. As you hold that tree in your mind, how do you feel? Is there another object in Nature which makes you feel the same way? Why do you suppose your reactions to these two objects are similar?

- What is your response to the threat of climate change? Are you fearful, angry, hopeful? Have you taken any steps to assume responsibility for your part in this global crisis?

Knowing the Way by Water

- Where is home for you? Is it where you live now, or is it some place where you once lived? Can you name three trees native to the place you call home? Can you name three resident birds? Do you know from which direction winter storms typically arrive? What impact does knowing (or not knowing) such facts have on your sense of 'home?'

- Could you create a map of your neighborhood from memory? Could you create a map of your neighborhood without reference to man-made objects?

- In this reflection, the author makes reference to *superstring theory* when she says, "Each proton is the united sparkling of quarks and photons, each of which is a sparkling. Of. Something." Does believing that all the particles and fundamental forces of Nature are linked together on a subatomic level change your experience of the place you inhabit?

Bones

- Choose one element of this reflection that particularly appeals to you and spend some time musing on it. How does this favorite portion change the way you see the world or the people around you?

- Do you have a favorite number? What is its significance for you? Where in Nature do you find that numerical pattern repeating?

- What landscape makes you feel most alive? Most centered? Most true to yourself? The mountains? The ocean? The desert? The woods?

Vigil

- In the Gospel of John we read, "In the beginning was the Word." How would your experience of creation change if you were to rephrase that to read, "In the beginning was the Dream"?

- In your own words, explain what the author means when she says, "Let us pray for something deeper than thought or desire: that Earth's own wanting will take hold of us, that Earth's own dream for herself will take shape within us."

- Can you see the stars at night where you live? If so, how do they make you feel? If not, do you miss them? When was the last time you saw the Milky Way? What was your response?

The Barn

- Do you think it's an exaggeration to say, "50,000 children will die of hunger today because you and I like to get where we're going fast and easy"? What is the relationship between consumerism and world hunger? What can we do to simplify our lives?

- In your own words, what does the barn in this reflection symbolize? Do you feel that your lifestyle distances you from "something vital"? What can you do to try to recapture that aliveness?

- Henry David Thoreau suggested that we, "Live each season as it passes, breathe the air, drink the drink, taste the fruit, and resign yourself to the influences of each." How might cultivating such an attitude lead to feelings of affection and solicitude for the Earth, or for your small corner of it?

In Praise of Surf

- The author spells out a "triune transmutation of energy" among earth, sea and sky. How would you explain that process in your own words?

o How do human beings participate in the "transmutation of energy" that is represented by the "tumbling, surging surf"?

> ACTIVITY TO SHARE: At your next meal, take a minute to recognize the various energies present before you – the animals whose flesh you're consuming, the plants, the sunlight, the water. Let each person name one way he or she will use that energy tomorrow.

o What sense do you make out of the author's equation between this "transmutation of energy" and what we call "love"? Does this affect your attitude towards the natural world in any way?

The Field

o Does it surprise you to realize that, at the atomic level, you have virtually no substance? Find something – a flower, a shell, a piece of tree bark – and spend a few minutes contemplating your connection to it at the atomic level. Do you notice any changes in your relationship with the natural world?

o When you think back over your life, can you identify times when you felt emotionally, psychologically or spiritually empty? What positive change emerged from your contact with that inner emptiness?

o Does your environment – neighborhood, house, kitchen – feel crowded? How might you empty your surroundings a bit, making them more conducive to "the holy nothingness that makes possible all our somethings"?

We Shall Be Changed

o Can you compare the feeling you get when you buy something new to the feeling you get when you witness a beautiful sunset? Is one more permanent than the other?

- It's been said that, "The cost of a thing is what you sacrifice in order to have it." What costs do you incur for convenience?

- What might you need to sacrifice in order to have a more intimate connection to Nature's beauty, wisdom and mystery?

Blue Moon

- In this reflection, the author describes an experience that makes her believe in "a silent tug on the strand of energy" linking her body to that of a heron. Have you ever had such an experience? If so, how would you go about repeating it? If not, how might you create such a "bridge" between yourself and some animate or inanimate being?

- *Superstring theory* holds that the universe is "an indivisible strand of energy in constant communication with itself." How does this fit in with your current religious or philosophical beliefs?

- In your own words, what is the "promise" of the universe we inhabit? Can you think of one small action you could take now that would contribute to that promise?

A Journey into Chesapeake Country

Like Thoreau's Walden Pond or Dillard's Tinker Creek, Ayres' Chesapeake Country is both place and metaphor. Herons and gulls, crabs and sea nettles, ghost ships and singing rocks... even barnacles can reveal those secret longings you hardly dare acknowledge, even to yourself. We hope this guide will help you explore both regions: Chesapeake Country and your own heart.

> To listen to sample recordings of this audiobook, visit
> www.CreativeWritingCenter.com/audiobooks/
> invitation-to-wonder-journey-series.

Bay Betrothal

- o Recall the last time you saw sunlight playing on the surface of a body of water. Or, if you live inland, think about sunlight sparkling on waves of wheat in fields, or dappling the leaves of trees, or glinting on the rock formations of a desert mesa. How does the interaction of light and landscape make you feel?

- o Male seahorses carry their offspring. Can you think of other species that do likewise? Identify one creature unique to the place where you live.

- o The author says, "We are, after all, improbable creatures, spirits wed to clay, divine sparks flung on the wood of this world in hopes of a fine, bright conflagration, or maybe it's a joyous dance our maker had in mind?" What do you think she means by that?

Barnacles and Tides

- o The barnacle possesses neither heart nor brain, yet it clearly demonstrates awareness of its environment. Looking past cats and dogs, have you ever had an experience of awareness or apparent intelligence in a non-human creature? Was there anything magical or mysteries about that encounter?

- o Like the turtle, the barnacle locks itself inside its shell for self-protection. What shell protects you? What allows you to open up again?

- o The author refers to the rhythms of the tide as a music that "belongs to all of us, no matter where we live." Can you name a way in which the movement of planetary tides affects your day-to-day existence?

Sea Nettles

- o In this reflection, the author identifies certain sounds and smells distinct to the pier where she's standing. Imagine yourself in a favorite place, present or past. What sounds and smells do you associate with that place?

- o The author describes a vivid memory from her childhood. What was it? Do you have a vivid outdoor memory from childhood?

    ACTIVITY TO SHARE: Have each person in your family describe a significant memory of the natural world. Create family outings to each of these special places. If the place is too far to visit in the immediate future, see if you can find a novel or movie set in that locale, then read or watch it together.

- o If you were to consult the child you once were about a problem you're experiencing right now, what would she or he say?

Blue Crab Etude

- o Do you have memories of your grandparents? Did they impart to you any valuable lessons?

- Crabbing is an activity indigenous to the Chesapeake Bay. What outdoor activities are indigenous to your region? Do you participate in them? Do you have any outstanding memories associated with these activities?

- The author says that life is "a perpetual tug 'o war" in which "a taut line is sometimes all we have of what we need." What do you think she means by that? Have there been times when "bait and prize" seemed indistinguishable to you? Have there been times of "too much resistance"? Do you agree with the author that "ceaseless effort is the cost of all things hoped for"?

The Gift

- In this reflection, the author describes in careful detail what it feels like to wade in water. When was the last time you took off your shoes to wade barefoot in… water, mud, grass, a plush carpet? How did it feel, taking time to savor this sensual delight?

- The author compares herself to an amphibian, "neither of the land nor of the sea but of both." In your life, do you ever seem to be straddling two worlds? What does this feel like?

- In your familial relationships, how do you hang onto "the submerged mystery" of your own psyche?

Fossils

- The author says, "20 million years ago, Southern Maryland was covered by a warm, shallow sea." Can you describe the forces active in your bioregion 20 million years ago? What traces remain?

- The author describes innumerable shades of black, brown and pink found in shells and rocks. How many shades of the same color can you find in Nature? (It might help to select a particular object, like leaves, bark or clouds.)

- o In this reflection the author suggests that humanity might one day outgrow its need for warfare. Do you agree? Do you think that the human species is evolving? Into what?

The Bridge

- o What changes has "progress" made in the place where you grew up? What are the benefits and negative consequences of these changes?

- o The writer Simone Weil says, "To be rooted is perhaps the most important but least understood need of the human soul." Does being outdoors help you assuage your need to be rooted? How?

- o In this reflection, the author compares human beings to a turtle which is "determined to fix his own destiny" yet is "utterly helpless." What does she mean by that? Do you agree? How might establishing greater intimacy with the natural world empower human beings to achieve their destiny?

Ghost Ship

- o Albert Einstein said, "Imagination is more important than knowledge." What do you think he meant by that?

- o Are you currently experiencing any longing to "break free"? What, in Nature, would symbolize your yearning? Is there someone in your life who could benefit from your imagining them to be "more than" they are now?

- o What are three things you could do to assuage Earth's hunger to become "one living, thriving, pulsing, begetting being"?

The Moon of My Belonging

- o Make a quick list of book, song or movie titles with the word 'moon' in them. How many did you come up with?

ACTIVITY TO SHARE: On the next full moon, have everyone in your family share lyrics to a song or words to a poem, about the moon. Make it a party! Invite your neighbors to celebrate the moon with you.

- o The author says, "This chunk of lifeless rock carries our hearts and longings with her on her 28 day journey." In what way is that true for you? What thoughts or feelings arise in you when you look up at the moon? Have you ever had a memorable encounter with a full moon?

- o What is your land of belonging? At what times are you particularly aware of your attachment to that place? If you don't feel attached to a place now, is there some landscape that *is* beckoning to you?

Keeper of the Light

- o Recall a recent news item that disturbed you. Now picture yourself in a storm at sea, and suddenly you see a lighthouse beacon. What effect, if any, does this active imagining have on your response to the news item?

- o When was the last time someone "made your day" with a small act of kindness? Were you inspired to "pass it on"?

- o Lighthouses are to coastal regions what windmills are to Holland. What structures emblemize *your* region?

A Different Kind of Wonderful

- o When you're at the beach, do you like to collect things? Can you recall one especially significant finding? How is that memory like wings?

- o The author invites you to "follow me into the luminescent air." As you listened to this reflection, did you feel inspired or uplifted in any way? Describe.

o The author describes a heron's call as, "Scrank, scrank." Pick several birds native to your region and try to put their calls into words.

> ACTIVITY TO SHARE: Before arriving at your next party, jot down the names of ten birds common to your area on index cards. As in "Charades," pass these out and have someone act out that bird's song, as others try to guess the bird's name.

Rock Chorus

o In this reflection, the author claims that rocks are singing. What about the rocks feels like music to the author? Have you ever had a similar experience with an inanimate object in the natural world?

o The *Song of Songs* claims that, "Love is stronger than death; vast flames cannot quench it nor rivers sweep it away." How is it that the planet Earth manifests an energy "stronger than death"? In your lifetime, have you experienced such resilience in Nature?

o Who is the "we" the author refers to when she says, "Whatever decisions we make, we make together"? Can you cite an instance of this "we" making a decision together? What kinds of choices does this "we" need to make in the future so that Earth can be healed?

A Journey into Divine Presence

The glory of the natural world slakes our thirst for the living God. A singing bird, a field of flowers, the liquid tattoo of waves on sand – such wondrous moments are a direct pipeline to divine presence. We hope this guide helps you discover new aspects of Nature's beauty, wisdom and mystery, and that as you open to the holiness that lies at the source of all being, you will find yourself joyfully embracing that which opens to enfold you.

> To listen to sample recordings of this audiobook, visit
> www.CreativeWritingCenter.com/audiobooks/
> invitation-to-wonder-journey-series

Raindrops in the River

- o In this reflection, the author describes a "figure-ground" experience with a roadside ditch. In your own words, explain what happened to her.

- o For the raindrop, life is eternal. It falls from the sky only to be swept back up into the sky and fall again. How do such enduring cycles in Nature affirm your experience of the divine?

- o Do you agree that "my me is God"? Why or why not?

Naming a Place Called Spring

- o Describe your first encounter with "earth's fecund and seductive mysteries." How old were you? How has this experience affected your life and/or your relationship with the divine?

    > ACTIVITY TO SHARE: Find a like-minded friend. Exchange "God memories" connected with the natural world. Make a pact: You'll talk in one week, each sharing a new experience of the divine in Nature's marvels.

- In this reflection, the author draws a parallel between "nibbling flowers" and the Christian sacrament of Holy Eucharist. Are you shocked or even offended by this comparison? How do you understand "communion" in your faith tradition? What aspects of Nature embody "communion" for you?

- Compare these two statements, the first from this reflection, the second from the writings of the 13th century theologian Meister Eckhart:
    "Once you name a thing, it becomes easy to substitute the word for the reality."
    "To seek God by rituals is to get the ritual and lose God."
    How does being outdoors in Nature take you beyond words and rituals?

What the Light Calls Forth

- The hymn "Morning Has Broken" says, "Mine is the sunlight, mine is the morning," and suggests we "praise God's recreation of the new day." How would it change your experience of creation and Creator to say, "*I am* the sunlight, *I am* the morning, *I am* the recreation of this new day"?

- Do you believe there is a separation between spirit and matter or do you see spirit as indwelling the process of creation? What do you think the author believes?

- Traditionally, Christian catechisms refer to God as "all knowing" and "all powerful." In this reflection, the author describes "Every pool and ditch, every mountain and valley, every animal, mineral, vegetable" as "a wholeness that the light calls forth, that beauty and truth proclaim, that omniscience asks us to know and omnipotence summons us to create." What is she suggesting with this comparison?

Woodswalk

- Many spiritual disciplines advocate being fully present in the "now" moment. How does this walk in the woods help the author become present in the "now"?

- Can you paraphrase the experience that makes the author say, "I am music, I am dance."

- The Jewish theologian Abraham Heschel wrote that, "Awareness of the divine begins with wonder." Can you recall an "encounter with wonder" you've had in Nature? Was it an experience of the divine? How?

The Gathering

- The Suquamish leader, Chief Seattle, said, "This we know: the earth does not belong to man, man belongs to the earth. All things are connected like the blood that unites us all." What aspects of "The Gathering" echo the statement attributed to Seattle?

- Picking blackberries becomes an intentionally religious act in this reflection. In what way? Can you recall a time when Nature inspired you to a similar religious experience?

- How might "gathering a sweet and secret nectar from each and every task" make one feel closer to God?

Mimosa Moment

- In this reflection, the author humorously describes a new religion she calls *Mimosa*. What are the basic tenets of that faith?

- Do you believe that after death your "soul will blossom into a surprise of potential"? What will that potential look like?

- Can you find one thing in your own backyard that could be called a "testament to the unlikely"? Can you find there one "astonishing witness" to possibility?

The Barn

- In your own words, what does the barn in this reflection symbolize? Do you feel that your lifestyle distances you from the sacred dimension of Nature? How might you recover that holiness?

- Author Richard Louv says, "We cannot care for God if we do not care for his creation." Do you agree? Why or why not?

- The Indian spiritual leader Mahatma Ghandi said we should, "Live simply that others might simply live." How might simplifying your own life affect "geopolitical, geosocial, geoeconomic" issues?

In Praise of Surf

- The author spells out a "triune transmutation of energy" among earth, sea and sky. How would you explain that process in your own words? What tenets of your own faith tradition are embodied in this "perpetuity of give and take."

- What sense do you make out of the author's equation between the "tumbling, surging surf" and what we call "love"? How is the one thing like the other? Have you ever felt loved by Nature?

- Recall the last time you were at the ocean. What about that experience would you call sacred? Could you somehow recreate such a sacred moment in your neighborhood?

Catching the Light

- Jesus Christ said, "Unless a grain of wheat falls to the earth and dies, it remains just a grain of wheat. But if it dies, it produces much fruit." How do the translucent stones of this reflection embody Christ's statement? If you are not a Christian, do the stones symbolize some aspect of your faith tradition?

o Kwanzaa, Christmas and Hanukkah have been around for 43, 1,673 and 2,174 years, respectively, but these feasts can remind us of an exclusive rather than an inclusive heritage. The solstice reminds us that we all share the sun's light. Celebrating it aligns us with mystery, with those forces at work throughout the universe that have guided and energized humanity for all of its several-million years history. How might you incorporate an awareness of the winter solstice into your family's holiday tradition?

ACTIVITY TO SHARE: If you send out holiday cards, make sure you include an acknowledgement of the solstice. You have the publisher's permission to use "The Fulcrum" in this book for that one purpose only, as long as you credit the author. Or download a picture of the sun, scrawl "Welcome back!" on it, and place the picture in every gift you give.

o In this reflection, the author draws a parallel between "light" and "love." Can you explain that connection in your own words? How have you experienced this "loving light"?

The Journey

o At the end of this reflection, the author says we will "meet, face to face, that from which we were fashioned. Our *alpha* and our *omega*, the sum of all our yearnings." What do those Greek words mean? How might that meaning be applied to stars and atoms?

o In the Christian tradition, Jesus Christ is often called the "alpha and omega." What is the author suggesting by comparing the planet Venus to Christ?

- o What other typically spiritual qualities – compassion, for instance – does matter exhibit in this reflection?

We Shall Be Changed

- o Christ said, "Where your treasure is, there your heart will be." What do the women in the exercise class treasure? In what ways are they representative of our culture?

- o The author says, "Earth, sea and sky seemed to meet in that moment, their boundaries softened as they offered themselves each to each to be reshaped, refashioned, changed." In your own words, explain why this is an essentially religious experience.

- o Just as people can be changed by contact with the natural world, they can be changed by constant exposure to shopping malls and asphalt. How are shopping malls and asphalt affecting you, your family, your country, your planet? What small steps could you take to reverse those consequences?

Rock Chorus

- o In this reflection, when the author holds glistening wet rocks in her hands, she thinks of phrases from the *Song of Songs* – "Set me like a seal on your heart," for example, and "Love is stronger than death." What implications do you draw from these juxtapositions?

- o Mysticism can be defined as "communion with or conscious awareness of an ultimate reality, divinity, spiritual truth, or God through direct experience." Have you ever had a mystical experience while outdoors?

> ACTIVITY TO SHARE: In "Rock Chorus," the author is awed by the fact that, "Some of my molecules were frozen in the ice of an ancient glacier." Gather a group of friends or family members and perform your own adaptation of "The Cosmic Walk," created by Sr. Miriam MacGillis of

Genesis Farm. Variations of this ritual can be found by Googling "cosmic walk genesis farm."

- o The author repeats a phrase, "fragments of a lost whole, ciphers for the eons." What is the lost wholeness to which she is referring? How can we recover it?

Still Night, Twin Moons

- o "For you alone my soul in silence waits." In this reflection, the author describes a shift in understanding the "you" of that phrase. What is the shift? How might such a change in understanding affect the current environmental crisis or other planetary issues we're facing now?

- o Author and peace activist Marianne Williamson says, "Our greatest fear is not that we are inadequate, but that we are powerful beyond measure." Where in this reflection does Ayres make the same point?

- o Can you cite moments in your life when weakness won out over strength? What about the life of your community, your nation? What hope for healing do the "twin moons" of this reflection represent?

Study Guide for Writers

The questions in this study guide originated with an online writing class offered at the Elizabeth Ayres Center for Creative Writing. (For more information on that class, visit www.CreativeWritingCenter.com/online-writing-course/the-writers-eye.) In *The Writer's Eye* course, through weekly themes, readings and writing prompts, aspiring writers learn to wield the power of thought, emotion and memory to cultivate a more imaginative response to their world. The course empowers writers to look at their lives with keener eyes, discovering the subtle nuances and surprising details that make any work of literature more memorable.

Since the questions form part of an assignment that is intended to be submitted in writing, you will get the most out of this guide if you write down your answers to the questions. You might want to dedicate a special notebook to that purpose.

The reflections appear here in the order in which they're treated in *The Writer's Eye* class, for the most part, but you could skip around if you want. The sequence is not important for purposes of this guide.

Rock Chorus

- Good writing always evokes a response in the reader. In this reflection, how does the author use images and sensory details to go beyond mere description ("this is what happened to me") so that readers can feel, 'This is happening to *me*'?

- If you can connect with your readers on the profound level of "I am part of the human species," rather than "I am a soccer player" or "I am the mother of three kids," you will have generated a strong and mysterious bond with your reader. In "Rock

Chorus," how does the introduction of the Biblical quotations take the reader into the territory of "this is bigger than me"?

A Different Kind of Wonderful

- o How do those ending questions, addressed directly to the reader, take the reflection to a transpersonal level where joy, fear, mystery and insight intersect?

Praising Green

- o What metaphor allows the author to make the scientific explanation of chlorophyll a direct, immediate experience for the reader?

- o How does paragraph four ("Ah, I understand now...") change the tone of the essay?

Bay Betrothal

- o How does the focus on the seahorse make the description of Nature more personal and intimate?

Woodswalk

- o How does the hyperbole of paragraph five ("Still at last...") serve that dictum so fundamental to good writing: "Show it, don't tell it."

Everything Curves

- o Surprise is an important part of the creative process, and it's also a fundamental element in any good writing, because anything that surprises your readers grabs their attention and invites them to enter into the space beyond the ordinary and quotidian. The author reports that she began "Everything Curves" with a comparison that was just a glimmer of insight: she knew Valentine's Day was coming up. She was struck with the curved shape of the traditional heart juxtaposed with the curves found everywhere in Nature. She had also been reading about the curvature of space and time. The surprise for her, while writing, was the last paragraph, where she was taken into a completely different kind of curvature than she had initially imagined. In your own words, what is the new insight of paragraph four ("Everything curves, it seems...")?

- o The opening sentence of paragraph four is a repetition of the first sentence of paragraph two. How does the repetition reinforce the twist of the ending?

Notes of a Native Daughter

- o The author reports that the inciting insight of this reflection was a connection she saw between a hole in the Chesapeake Bay and a hole she feels exists in the American psyche as a result of genocide and slavery. She was writing at the time President Obama was being inaugurated the first time, and the surprise for her was discovering a way to connect the two holes with Obama's election. Comment on the author's use of the "journal that is my heart" imagery. How does it serve the purpose of the reflection?

Butterfly Q and A

- o The author reports that she wanted to write about honeysuckle – that was what was calling to her at the time: honeysuckle was in bloom; she was transfixed by the smell. But she also knew this essay would be published in her newspaper column in July, so she related honeysuckle to Independence Day. What impact does the connection between "nectar" and "freedom" make on the reader?

Blue Crab Etude

- o Memory is a powerful point of connection between author and reader, but it's important that the writer allow the reader into the memory (as opposed to making it overly me-centered, which can exclude the reader). In "Blue Crab Etude," how does the author evoke childhood memories and make them more than just "this is what happened to me when I was a kid"?

- o What words or phrases or sensory details conjure up a sense of place in this reflection?

Fossils

- o How does the author evoke "deep time" (a sense of bygone epochs) in this reflection?

- o How do the "deep time" references contribute to the reader's experience of place (thereby transcending merely personal memory on the part of the author)?

- o In paragraph seven ("After a few tries..."), how would you say the various colors are affecting the author's sensibilities?

- o If you were to put the author's reaction to the colors described in this paragraph into your own words, what would her reaction be? (Be playful here! Maybe "wowie-zowie" would sum it up nicely!)

- o In the very last paragraph ("I am for home now..."), how does the author make use of the color 'green'?

The Moon of My Belonging

- o How do the metaphors of "family" and "inheritance" transcend the merely personal experience of the author, giving readers a sense of intimacy with the moon and with the place where this particular moon shines?

Thanksgiving Hallelujah

- o Much of the impact of this reflection depends on a fundamental comparison that moves from a primary simile (the colors of autumn are like a fire) to another imaginative use of fire in its literal meaning – the fire around which people might gather. How does the author create the "colors of autumn are like a fire" experience for you?

o In paragraph four ("No painter could ever do justice…"), how does she make the science of color a "show it, don't tell it" experience for you?

We Shall Be Changed

o In paragraph four ("Their obvious and passionate longing shocked me…"), the author uses the color white to set up visual "echoes." Describe that "echoed imagery" in your own words.

o What is the impact on the reader of those reverberating images?

The Field

o The author reports that when she started writing about her Chesapeake Bay homeland, she wanted her readers to experience the feelings of amazement she was experiencing. She became curious about the science underlying the natural world and was surprised to find that the scientific underpinnings of the universe (e.g., evolution, quantum physics) had become numinous for her. She was smitten by what might be called the "wow" factor in scientific fact. Begin by identifying one small scientific fact that "wows" you. For instance, "the whooping crane has an 8 foot wingspan." Or, "The monarch butterfly migrates thousands of miles." Or, "The human eye evolved from the chlorophyll molecule." Or, "The human species is the result of a 4.5 billion year earth history." Identify your fact, and write a paragraph that communicates your fascination therewith.

o In "The Field," how does the emptiness of the atom become a comment on contemporary culture?

- How does the author turn this emptiness into a "wow" for the reader? What phrases or lines make it evocative?

Knowing the Way by Water

- How does the author utilize the scientific fact that water is composed of two molecules of hydrogen and one molecule of oxygen?

- What's the impact, the "wow factor," on the reader?

What the Light Calls Forth

- In paragraph three ("Scientists also say...") the author writes, "My head can't wrap itself around these facts but my heart whispers 'I knew it all along.'" Can you comment on how this avoidance of complex scientific exegesis helps the reader experience a "wow factor"?

Vigil

- How does the author's personal yearning to see stars transcend the personal and become a collective yearning?

Clouds

- Point out the various ways in which the author uses the metaphor of "clouds are words."

- What impact does this have on the reader?

- Comment on the impact of "skewing" grammar in paragraph one ("...if I. Just. Look. Up."); in paragraph two ("Anyway. They. Can."); and, in paragraph five ("...if we would only. Look. Up."

Prequel to Autumn

- In the first paragraph, the author writes, "Out, down, cross, up, out, down, then: from that dither of flopping legs and flapping arms I glance out the window to see a single black crow streak upward into the lapis lazuli air." What is the impact on the reader of the sighting of the crow?

o The beginning of paragraph three ("For me, the sky is shorthand...") shifts the focus of the essay from what to what?

o Do you relate to the author's statement that denizens of the air are "messengers"?

Ghost Ship

o In paragraph two ("As I sit..."), the author moves into an imaginative reverie. First, re-tell the reverie in your own words, then describe the impact it has on the reader.

o How would you articulate – in your own words – the "groping to become more than" described in paragraph three ("Sure, and don't you agree...")?

o In your own words, what is "the ghostly existence we are trapped in"? What is the author's vision for the future of the planet, as evoked in the last paragraph of the reflection?

The Pier

o In this reflection, the wind ends up becoming a metaphor for planetary unification. In one paragraph, re-tell the steps that lead to that conclusion, citing specific transitional phrases.

o How does the author use her personal experience of the beach in paragraph five ("And the beach remembers...") to make a cultural observation?

In Praise of Surf

o With what words or phrases does the author make the equation between "surf" and "love"?

- From a literary point of view, what is the impact on the reader of the repetition of the language from paragraph three ("These waves...") in paragraph six ("In all your hours...")?

- Explain how, in this reflection, the rhythm of surf is imitated in the language of the reflection. Cite specific phrases.

- Focusing on paragraphs four, five and six, make a list of the more metaphoric ways in which qualities of surf, of waves crashing on shore, are used in the reflection.

Song Flows Forth

- How many different "springs" does the author allude to? How does she establish unity among them?

Raindrops in the River

- This reflection expresses a certain mystical realization on the part of the author. In your own words, explain that realization. Would you apply the word 'mystical' to it? Why or why not?

- Paragraph one introduces a phrase descriptive of raindrops: tat, tat, tat. In the last sentence of the essay, the phrase is repeated. To what does it now refer? What is the impact on the reader of repeating this phrase?

Prequel to Winter

- In your own words, what is "the work of winter" as the author conveys it?

- In terms of the "show it, don't tell it" practicum, how does the author evoke an experience of winter for the reader?

Reconciling with April

- 'April' can be the name of a person or the name of a month. How does the author play on that ambiguity in this reflection?

- o In your own words, what work does April accomplish in the mind and heart of the author?

The Gathering

- o How many different kinds of 'gatherings' are going on in this reflection? Please list them.

- o In your own words, explain the work the author is engaged in. What phrases make her experience engaging to the reader?

- o What happens in the last paragraph of the reflection to move the reader from actual to imagined experience? What does this imaginative leap do for the reader?

Remembering the Future

- o The theme of the assignment in which this reflection is studied is "witness," used as a verb: "to give evidence of, to testify to." In your own words, explain the truth to which the author bears witness in this reflection.

- o What is the literary impact of the discovery of the feathers in paragraph seven ("That blustery afternoon....")? Does this change the tone of the essay for you?

The Barn

- o How does the lifestyle of the homesteaders as described herein bear witness to a truth the author obviously wishes us all to emulate?

- o A phrase was introduced in the first paragraph: "with muscle and purpose." When the phrase appears in the last paragraph, its meaning has changed. Please explain the shift in meaning.

Still Night, Twin Moons

- o The author uses the metaphor of a palindrome to say something about how she experiences her relationship to the divine. Can you explain her perception in your own words? Do you share that perception?

- o What metaphor would you use to express your relationship to the divine?

Catching the Light

- o What imagery does the author use that "catches the light" for you?

- o How does she change the connotation of the word "light" in the last paragraph?

- o What is the relationship between the literal stones discussed in paragraph two ("Then I saw them...") and the metaphoric "stones" of human experience discussed in paragraph five ("This Christmas morning...")?

The Journey

- o What imagery does the author use to convey sunset? Sunrise?

- o At what point in the reflection does the author move from talking about a literal river to talking about a more metaphoric river, the "river of time"? How does she use scientific facts to make that transition?

Baking for the Holidays

- o Paragraphs two, three and four of this essay contain a condensed treatment of the contrast between light and dark. In a few sentences, and in your own words, how does the author experience the difference between light and darkness?

The Gift

- The idea of wings and flight only appears at the very end of "The Gift," and yet it changes the trajectory of the reflection completely. Comment on that shift.

- How does the first paragraph evoke a sensory experience of walking on a grassy path?

- How does paragraph two use language to create a sense of encounter with the water?

- In paragraphs three, four and five, what words or phrases evoke the sensory experience of wading?

- In what ways does the heron become a metaphor? (In other words, what does the image of the heron represent to the author? To you?)

The Fulcrum

- In your own words, restate the "argument" of this reflection.

- What point is the author making about the winter solstice as a metaphor for conscious evolution?

Blue Moon

- In this reflection, the author refers to superstring theory, which she defines in paragraph two. In your own words, explain how her encounter with the heron embodies the fact that "we're all connected" at the subatomic level.

- How does the blue moon become a metaphor for connection?

Prequel to Winter

- This reflection is about befriending that which initially seems difficult or inimical (i.e., the season of winter). In your own words, re-state the transformation the author experiences.

- What words or phrases most vividly express what the author feels she's learning from winter?

- What role in her changed attitude is played by the leafless tree limbs? What is the function of the last image, the flock of small birds?

Seedsong: An Elegy

- An elegy is a poetic form that praises the dead, and this meditation extends the meaning of the form to include prose. Based on your reading, what did Thomas Berry cherish? Why did the author value her relationship with him?

- In the opening paragraph, what is the impact of the phrase "mountains leaned into each other like sorrowing friends"?

- In the third paragraph ("White mushrooms dot…"), what is the effect on the reader of this comparison: "A network of exposed roots meanders, like the ropey veins on an old man's hands"?

- The author directly addresses the departed, not once but twice, at the end of the third paragraph and at the beginning of the fourth paragraph. What is the impact on the reader of this direct address? What is the effect of its being repeated?

- In this reflection, how does loss transform itself into a celebration of life?

- Experiment with writing an elegy yourself.

Keeper of the Light

- o The opening paragraph describes a certain energy apparent in the natural elements. What words or phrases create the effect of disturbance?

- o In your own words, describe the author's response to the reality of cataclysm, in Nature and in world events.

Barnacles and Tides

- o In paragraph one, with what words or phrases does the author move the reader from an above-ground to a below-water experience?

- o In paragraph two, how do the sounds contribute to a feeling of being underwater?

- o In paragraph three, what holds the reader's attention on the barnacles?

Shadows

- o List all the similes and descriptive phrases the author uses to describe shadows.

- o Put your commentary into practice. Choose any three sounds that pop into your mind. Brainstorm five similes or descriptive phrases for each. Go nuts! Get crazy! Let your imagination run wind!

  For example, the sound of crickets could be...

  1. Musicians tuning up for autumn's symphony;
  2. Stars hiding themselves in the trees disguised as sound;
  4. Tiny drums made by fairies;
  5. A tintinnabulate chorus.

Joe's Garden

- o In paragraph four, the reader discovers that the garden in question has its roots in history, because "the land was settled long before we arrived." How does this shift your perspective on the garden Joe has planted?

- o How does the author's perspective change when she imagines, "I am the ancestor who wielded it..."?

Mimosa Moment

- o What imagery does the author use to convey the wonders of the mimosa blossoms? What about the scent of the flowers, how does she convey that?

- o What effect does the hyperbole (a new religion called 'Mimosa') have on the reader? How does the hyperbole serve to communicate the author's experience of the mimosa blooms?

- o The paragraph that begins "Tight green knobs...." looks closely at the buds of the mimosa flower. How is that imagery used to speak of death?

ELIZABETH AYRES is the author of three other books: *Home After Exile, Writing the Wave* and *Swimming the River of Stone*, as well as the audiobook series *Creative Writing from A to Z* and the audiobooks in the *Invitation to Wonder 'Journey' Series,* which are based on *Mirror of Our Becoming.* She lives in Maryland's Chesapeake Bay area, where she paces shell-strewn beaches to pluck words from the soft salt breeze.

Ayres holds a Master's degree in Creative Writing from Syracuse University, where she was a Cornelia Ward Fellow. She's been hailed by *New York* magazine, *New York Newsday* and the *Village Voice* for her groundbreaking teaching methods. A charismatic workshop leader for over 40 years, Ayres has taught at New York University and the College of New Rochelle; at the New York Open Center and Ghost Ranch Conference Center; through Poets-in-the-Schools and Poets & Writers; in libraries and other public forums. In 1990, she founded the Elizabeth Ayres Center for Creative Writing, which offers retreats, online workshops and private instruction to a global community of aspiring writers.

Elizabeth Ayres can be contacted through her website: www.CreativeWritingCenter.com.

www.ingramcontent.com/pod-product-compliance
Lightning Source LLC
Chambersburg PA
CBHW020757160426
43192CB00006B/359